The Last Hours with Jesus

The Last Hours with Jesus
The Jerusalem Passion Play

Photography by Max and Hilla Jacoby
Text by Lawrence F. Mihlon

Doubleday & Company, Inc., Garden City, New York, 1982

For Sally
and those remarkable people
of Mount Zion Way,
my mother and father.

—L. F. M.

To the inhabitants of Jerusalem and to Mayor Teddy Kollek, the blessed rebuilder of Jerusalem—*He gives the freedom to all Who feel the urge to worship the Lord, Each and every one in his own way....*

Yahweh Sabaoth says this.
Now I am going to save my people
from the countries of the East
and from the countries of the West.
I will bring them back
to live inside Jerusalem.   Zechariah 8:7–8

—M. and H. J.

This book was made possible through the courtesy of Frank Parsons and *The Jerusalem Passion Play.*

Instrumental in the production of the Play and the Book are Producer-Director Francisco de Araujo, and Assistant Director Gregory Strom, who also has the role of Jesus. Credit is also due Rochelle Zaltzman for Costume Design, Schlomo Leibowitz for Set Design, Fakhury Brothers of Hebron for Pottery, and Tel Ad Studios of Jerusalem for Technical Design.

Library of Congress Catalog Card Number 81-43750
ISBN 0-385-18085-3

Photographs copyright © 1982 by Max Jacoby and Hilla Jacoby
Text copyright © 1982 by Lawrence F. Mihlon

First Edition
Printed in the United States of America

Introduction

The Jerusalem Passion Play and its companion production, the Bethlehem Nativity Play, offer audiences unforgettable nights of theater, great and glorious music, dance, and inspired acting. They are pageant and pageantry, combining the most modern sound-and-light technology with the most ancient surroundings. That the plays are presented on the very sites of the birth and death of Jesus leaves one palpitating in expectation and breathless at the experience.

As with the stories that took place in each city, the locations themselves are special. In Bethlehem, the Church of the Nativity conveys from its silent and vaulted rooms the sense of him, while Shepherds Field is the place of the flocks to this day. But it is Jerusalem that is unique.

Jerusalem is as much the crossroads of our civilization today as it was two thousand years ago. Only the most jaded creature among us can fail to pause in amazement at the knowledge that, in Jerusalem, one's feet do tread the same stones that Jesus walked and David defended. Wonder grows as one discovers that Jerusalem is also a thoroughly modern city with every convenience and requirement of modern life.

It is a beautiful city to behold visually, as well. Broad

avenues, banked with green. Narrow streets, winding through history. Even residential streets that could be in the finer sections of Paris or Rome. There seem to be gardens and parks everywhere.

Then there is the Old City, the actual City of David. If the entire city is too much to grasp, the impact of the Old City is beyond reach. The concentration of human history that one sees here sends the imagination soaring. Calvary, the Western Wall, Golgotha, the Via Dolorosa, the Temple Mount; all of the Holy Places, the holiest of places to Christian and Jew. A city and national government devoted to their preservation has been relentless in its digging, rebuilding, and restoring of these places, for all who would come to Jerusalem to wonder and worship.

Jerusalem is a city that is almost unbearably difficult to embrace. Too much has happened there. Too much continues to happen there. And too much will continue to happen there, according to the Bible. It is written that when Jesus comes again, it will be to Jerusalem.

But it is Jesus himself that the Jerusalem Passion Play and the Bethlehem Nativity Play are about, not the cities. If it is difficult for us to embrace the history and beauty of Jerusalem, it has been even more difficult for us to comprehend Jesus, who walked there and died there.

Jesus was and is a jumble of often disturbing contradictions.

He is the supreme symbol of love among men, and he has been for some two thousand years. No other figure in the history of mankind is remembered with the intensity of emotion with which that dear man is remembered.

As the likeness of Helen of Troy launched a thousand ships, the soul and spirit of Jesus launched the search for peace and understanding among all of us. But, because we have not always understood his message, the peace and understanding we seek continue to elude us. As Max Jacoby has said, he can only be weeping, there in Heaven, at our transgressions and at our distortions of his message. The hypocrisy of so many who carry his glorious banner before them as they brutalize the hearts and labor of others can only cause agony to him, perhaps greater agony than his last hours in Gethsemane.

He was a simple carpenter whose followers were but fishermen and plain folk as simple as he. He preached a simple message to a world complicated, even then, by preoccupation with self and the trappings of material power. Today, in a world become even more complicated and cynical, his message of love continues to confound us.

Jesus cared little for the politics of the day or the socio-economic milieu in which he preached. He was a Jew, preaching to other Jews and to whoever else would listen. We do not know what he did in those years between the flight to Egypt and the time he began his ministry, at age thirty. Perhaps it does not matter. What does matter is his ministry and the message of love it carries.

He died not because he wanted to die — otherwise his prayer in the Garden or his calling out on the Cross would not have asked, *"Eli, Eli, lama sabachthani?"* (My God, my God, why have you deserted me?") He died because there was no other way for God's word to be kept alive among those generations that were yet to come.

The story of his last hours on earth, his passion, is the most graphic and poignant drama ever written. There are no heroics in the classic sense. He wore no armor. He carried no sword. He commanded no army. His weapons were a few words, and no words. His protection was his anguish and his pure heart. He commanded only his spirit.

He died, to be sure. But through his resurrection he became more alive than those he left behind. He lives through them and through all of us always — "Yes, to the end of time."

The Birth and Passion of Jesus

This is how Jesus Christ came to be born. His mother Mary was betrothed to Joseph, but before they came to live together she was found to be with child through the Holy Spirit. Her husband Joseph, being a man of honor and wanting to spare her publicity, decided to divorce her informally. He had made up his mind to do this when the angel of the Lord appeared to him in a dream and said, "Joseph son of David, do not be afraid to take Mary home as your wife, because she has conceived what is in her by the Holy Spirit. She will give birth to a son and you must name him Jesus, because he is the one who is to save his people from their sins." Now all this took place to fulfill the words spoken by the Lord through the prophet: *The virgin will conceive and give birth to a son and they will call him Immanuel,* a name which means "God-is-with-us."

Matthew 1:18–23

The angel Gabriel was sent by
God to a town in Galilee called
Nazareth, to a virgin betrothed
to a man named Joseph, and the
virgin's name was Mary. "Listen!
You are to conceive and bear a
son, and you must name him
Jesus. . . . He will rule over the
House of Jacob for ever and his
reign will have no end."

Luke 1:26 – 33

"For nothing is impossible to God."

"I am the handmaid of the Lord," said Mary. "Let what you have said be done to me."

Mary set out at that time and went as quickly as she could to a town in the hill country of Judah.

Luke 1:37–39

She went into Zechariah's house
and greeted Elizabeth. Now as
soon as Elizabeth heard Mary's
greeting, the child leaped in her
womb and Elizabeth was filled
with the Holy Spirit. She gave a
loud cry and said, "Of all women
you are the most blessed, and
blessed is the fruit of your
womb."

Luke 1:40–42

Now at this time Caesar
Augustus issued a decree for a
census of the whole world to be
taken.

Luke 2:1

So Joseph set out from the town
of Nazareth in Galilee and
traveled up to Judaea . . . together
with Mary . . .

Luke 2:4,5

. . . there was no room for them
at the inn.

Luke 2:7

. . . there were shepherds who lived in the fields and took it in turns to watch their flocks during the night. The angel of the Lord appeared to them and the glory of the Lord shone around them.

Luke 2:8,9

"Do not be afraid. Listen, I bring you news of great joy, a joy to be shared by the whole people."

Luke 2:10

"You see this child: he is
destined for the fall and for the
rising of many in Israel, destined
to be a sign that is rejected . . ."

Luke 2:34

. . . some wise men came to
Jerusalem from the east. Herod
summoned the wise men to see
him privately.

Matthew 2:2,7

Having listened to what the king had to say, they set out. And there in front of them was the star they had seen rising; it went forward and halted over the place where the child was.

Matthew 2:9

The sight of the star filled them
with delight . . .

Matthew 2:10

and going into the house they
saw the child with his mother
Mary, and falling to their knees
they did him homage.

Matthew 2:11

Then, opening their treasures,
they offered him gifts of gold and
frankincense and myrrh.

Matthew 2:11

But they were warned in a
dream not to go back to Herod,
and returned to their own
country by a different way.

Matthew 2:12

Herod was furious when he
realized that he had been
outwitted . . .

Matthew 2:16

... and in Bethlehem and its
surrounding district he had all
the male children killed who
were two years old or under ...

Matthew 2:16

Prepare a way for the Lord,
make his paths straight.
Every valley will be filled in,
every mountain and hill be laid
low,
winding ways will be
straightened
and rough roads made smooth.
And all mankind shall see the
salvation of God.

Luke 3:4,5

"The Father loves me, because I lay down my life in order to take it up again. No one takes it from me; I lay it down of my own free will, and as it is in my power to lay it down, so it is in my power to take it up again; and this is the command I have been given by my Father."

John 10:17–18

. . . on his way to Jerusalem.
They took branches of palm and
went out to meet him, shouting,
"Hosanna! Blessings on the King
of Israel, who comes in the name
of the Lord."

John 12:13–14

. . . a woman came to Jesus with an alabaster jar of the most expensive ointment, and poured it on his head as he was at table. When they saw this, the disciples were indignant; "Why this waste?" they said.

Matthew 26:7,8

" . . . she did it to prepare me for
burial . . . wherever in all the
world this Good News is
proclaimed, what she has done
will be told also . . ."

Matthew 26:12,13

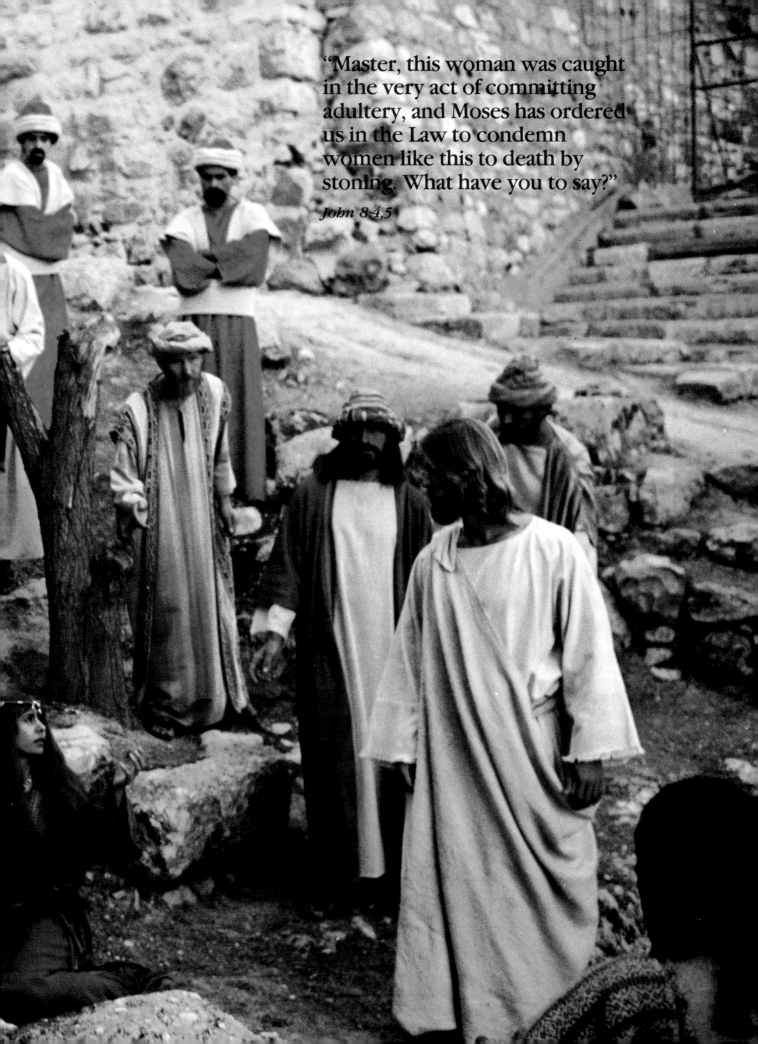

"Master, this woman was caught
in the very act of committing
adultery, and Moses has ordered
us in the Law to condemn
women like this to death by
stoning. What have you to say?"

John 8:4,5

Jesus bent down and started
writing on the ground with his
finger. He looked up and said, "If
there is one of you who has not
sinned, let him be the first to
throw a stone at her."

John 8:6,7

Martha said to Jesus, "If you had been here, my brother [Lazarus] would not have died." . . . Jesus wept; and the Jews said, "See how much he loved him!". . . he cried in a loud voice, "Lazarus, here! Come out!" The dead man came out . . . Jesus said to them, "Unbind him, let him go free."

John 11:21–44

Then Judas Iscariot went to the chief priests and said, "What are you prepared to give me if I hand him over to you?" They paid him thirty silver pieces, and from that moment he looked for an opportunity to betray him.

Matthew 26:14–16

" The Son of Man is going to his
fate, as the scriptures say he will,
but alas for that man by whom
the Son of Man is betrayed! "

Matthew 26:24

"Take it and eat, this is my body. . . . Drink all of you from this, for this is my blood, the blood of the covenant, which is to be poured out for many for the forgiveness of sins."

Matthew 26:26 – 28

"From now on, I shall not drink wine until the day I drink the new wine with you in the kingdom of my Father."

Matthew 26:29

At the Mount of Olives Jesus said to them, "You will all lose faith in me this night." . . . At this, Peter said, "Though all lose faith in you, I will never lose faith." Jesus answered him, "This very night, before the cock crows, you will have disowned me three times."

Matthew 26:31–34

Then Jesus came with them to
Gethsemane and . . . he prayed.
"My Father, if it is possible, let
this cup pass me by.
Nevertheless, let it be as you, not
I, would have it."

Matthew 26:36,39

The second and the third time he prayed, "If this cup cannot pass by without my drinking it, your will be done!"

Matthew 26:42

"You can sleep on now and take your rest. Now the hour has come when the Son of Man is to be betrayed into the hands of sinners.

"Get up! Let us go! My betrayer is already close at hand."

Matthew 26:45,46

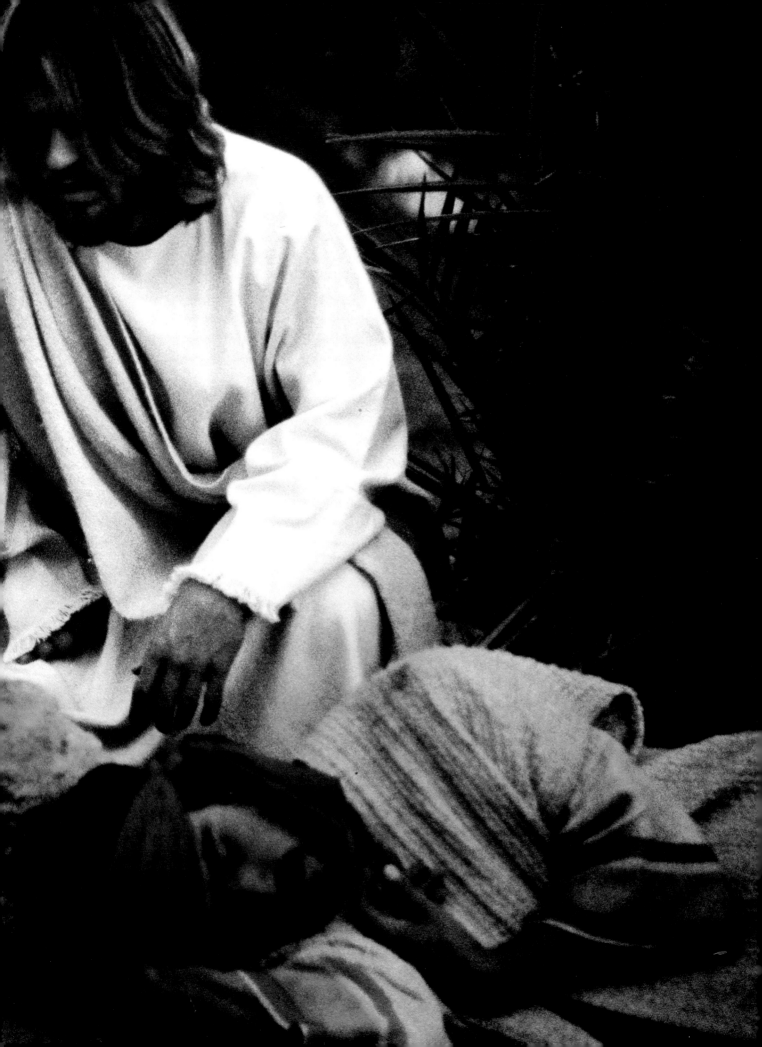

So he went straight up to Jesus and said, "Greetings, Rabbi," and kissed him. Jesus said to him, "My friend, do what you are here for."

Matthew 26:49,50

Then they came forward, seized
Jesus and took him in charge.

Matthew 26:50

The high priest then stood up and said to him, "What is this evidence these men are bringing against you?" But Jesus was silent.

Matthew 26:62,63

The men who had arrested Jesus led him off to Caiaphas the high priest, where the scribes and the elders were assembled. Peter followed him at a distance, and when he reached the high priest's palace, he went in and sat down with the attendants to see what the end would be.

Matthew 26:57,58

They said to Peter, "You are one of them for sure!" Then he started calling down curses on himself and swearing, "I do not know the man." At that moment the cock crew.

Matthew 26:73,74

Peter went outside and wept
bitterly.

Matthew 26:75

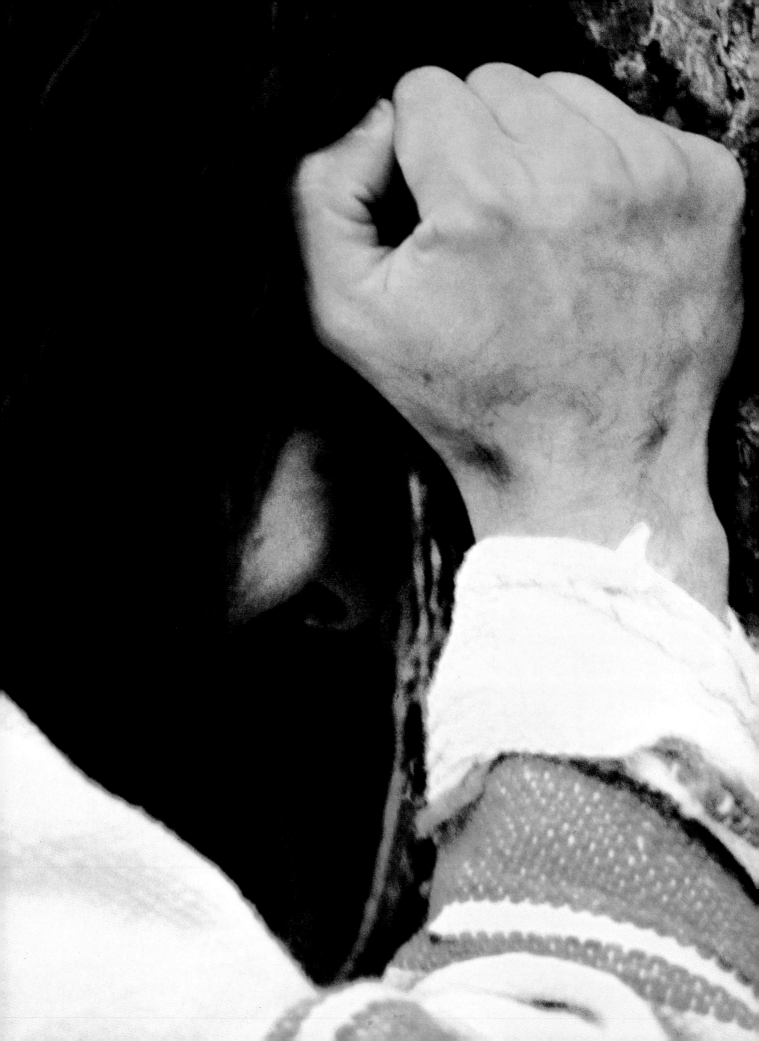

Jesus, then, was brought before
the governor, and Pilate put to
him this question, "Are you the
King of the Jews?" Jesus replied,
"It is you who say it."

Matthew 27:11

Now as he was seated in the chair of judgment, Pilate's wife sent him a message, "Have nothing to do with that man; I have been upset all day by a dream I had about him."

Matthew 27:19

So he took some water, washed
his hands in front of the crowd
and said, "I am innocent of this
man's blood. It is your concern."

Matthew 27:24

Pilate ordered Jesus to be first scourged and then handed over to be crucified. The governor's soldiers took Jesus with them into the Praetorium and collected the whole cohort around him.

Matthew 27:26,27

No longer was he protected. His
nobility and godlike bearing
goaded them to madness. His
meekness, his innocence, his
majestic patience filled them
with hatred.

Narrator, Passion Play

Tormentors! Stay your hands.
Are not your hearts with pity
moved, to see such anguish
meekly borne? Have pity. Stay
your hands.

Evangelist, Passion Play

Then they stripped him and made him wear a scarlet cloak, and having twisted some thorns into a crown they put this on his head and placed a reed in his right hand.

Matthew 27:28,29

When he found that Jesus had been condemned, Judas took the thirty silver pieces back and said, "I have betrayed innocent blood."

Matthew 27:3,4

He went and hanged himself.

Matthew 27:6

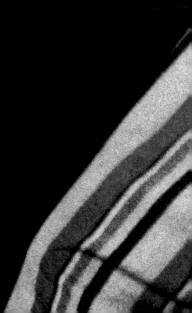

And carrying his own cross he
went out of the city to the place
of the skull or, as it was called in
Hebrew, Golgotha . . .

John 19:17

. . . where they crucified him.

John 19:18

Seeing his mother and the disciple he loved standing near her, Jesus said to his mother, "Woman, this is your son." After this to fulfill the scripture perfectly he said: "I am thirsty."

John 19:26,28

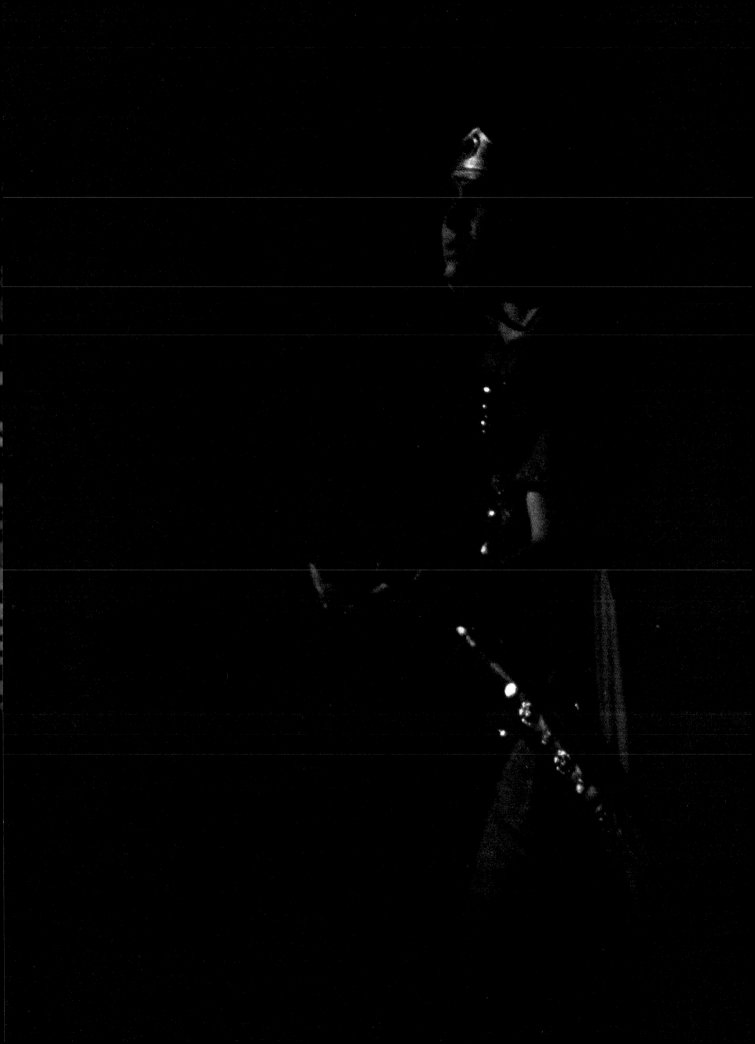

In truth this man was a son of
God.

Mark 15:39

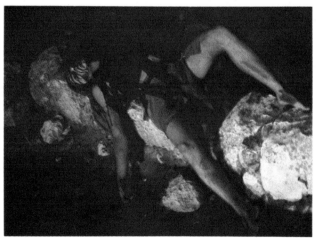

When it was evening, there
came a rich man of Arimathaea,
called Joseph, who had himself
become a disciple of Jesus. This
man went to Pilate and asked for
the body of Jesus.

Matthew 27:57,58

All at once there was a violent
earthquake, for the angel of the
Lord, descending from heaven,
came and rolled away the stone
. . . His face was like lightning.
The guards were so shaken . . .
Filled with awe and great joy,
the women came quickly away
from the tomb and ran to tell the
disciples.

Matthew 28:2 – 8

He is not here; he has risen.
Hallelujah!

Luke 24:6

So you see how it is written that the Christ would suffer and on the third day rise from the dead, and that, in his name, repentance for the forgiveness of sins would be preached to all the nations, beginning from Jerusalem.

Luke 24:46,47

Where Jesus Walked

Jesus was born in Bethlehem of Judea in a manger, because there was no room in the inn. Over that very place rises the Basilica of the Church of the Nativity. Beneath the manger (facing page) lies the Grotto of the Nativity, which one reaches by curved steps. Here one finds the Silver Star (above) that marks the spot of Jesus' birth. The church itself fairly dominates the architecture of

Bethlehem, a township of some 30,000 Christian Arabs. Many of them still pursue the arts and crafts of biblical days and fill the town's shops with their colorful wares. This place of so many memories was also where, 4,000 years ago, Jacob buried his young wife Rachel and later David was anointed by Samuel "in the midst of his brethren."

Shimmering in the sun, as it did some 3,000 years ago, is the City of David, the Old City of Jerusalem (above). After he captured the city, David brought the Ark of the Law to his home. With the Ark enshrined there, Jerusalem has become the eternal spiritual center of the Jewish people. Christians revere the Holy City for many reasons as well. At the Church of St. Peter en Gallicantu, for example, one finds the very steps (right) that Jesus would have used on the way to the Garden of Gethsemane after the Last Supper.

Along the eastern wall of the Old City and not far from the Tomb of the Virgin Mary is Lions' Gate (above). It is named after the two carved lions above either side of the entrance. Eastward from Jerusalem is the city of Jericho where Jesus fasted forty days. The well seen here (top) could have slaked the Lord's thirst.

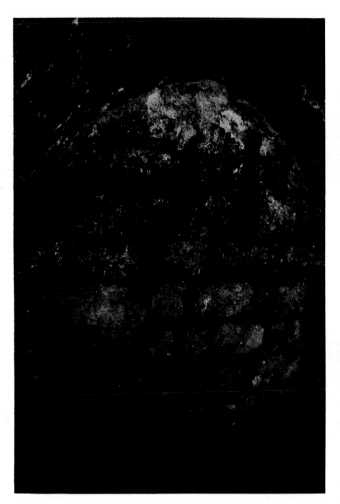

Continuing eastward from Jerusalem a traveler will come to the town of Bethany, where Jesus visited with his friend Lazarus and his two sisters. The place of Lazarus' tomb (above), from which he was restored to life by Jesus, rests in the courtyard behind the Sanctuary of St. Lazarus, a Franciscan monastery. The land around Jerusalem, the land of Israel, abounds with hills and valleys whose very rises and folds conjure biblical history. Here (right) we see the Valley of the Prophets.

Along the road to Bethlehem the traveler from Jerusalem bears witness to a countryside virtually unchanged since the days when Jesus and his followers walked this way.

"For out of Zion shall go forth the law, and the word of the Lord from Jerusalem." So said the prophet Isaiah about the place (left) we call Mt. Zion. Revered by Jews, Christians, and Muslims, it was the site of the first season of performances of the Jerusalem Passion Play. In West Jerusalem there has been built a 1:50 scale model of Jerusalem of the Second Temple. This remarkable construction is complete to the last detail. Here we see (right) the Temple itself. The model enables us to compare the Holy City as it was with the Old City of today.

From the site of the
Jerusalem Passion
Play we look across
the Kidron Valley
toward the Mount of
Olives (top). Rising
from its heights is the
Ascension Tower of
the Russian Church,
while just below it is
the Jerusalem
Panorama Hotel
where Francisco de
Araujo and his troupe
held their opening
and closing night
celebrations. To the
north is the Garden of
Gethsemane where
Jesus prayed three
times. Dominating the
garden are the ancient
olive trees, said to

have grown from
shoots of those trees
that were there 2,000
years ago.

When Jesus sat with
his disciples at the
Passover Seder table,
his Last Supper, it was
at the place on Mt.
Zion where now
stands the Dormition
monastery. In it is the
"large upper room"
(above).

Betrayed by Judas and arrested, Jesus began his sad journey to Calvary. One of the fourteen Stations of the Cross venerated to this day is the Church of the Flagellation. On its stone floor (left) Jesus suffered his scourging at the hands of Roman soldiers. Knowing his treachery had caused it all, Judas went and hanged himself at a place thought to be on this hill (right), called by many the Field of Blood.

From this place (left) there was no escape the night before his crucifixion. Preserved at the Church of St. Peter en Gallicantu, the dungeon also held actor Greg Strom the night before his first performance as Jesus in the Passion Play. Jesus' life ended at Golgotha, the place of the skull (top). And then, according to many Christians, he was laid to rest in the Garden Tomb (right), a place today not far from the Damascus Gate, along the North Wall of the Old City of Jerusalem.

The Story Behind the Play

The day of the last performance in the premier season of the Jerusalem Passion Play dawned with clouds that had blown in from the distant Mediterranean Sea. It was October 31, the day before the beginning of the winter season in the Holy Land. From November 1 through the month of March, rain would fall frequently on the hills and valleys that give Jerusalem much of its physical character. Welcome to the people of the city as the rain would be for its restorative kiss to the parched land, the valiant creators of the Passion Play prayed that the rain would not come too soon.

A sellout crowd was expected that night. And after more than six months of punishing work and extraordinary devotion to an ideal, everyone in the company was bone-weary and emotionally spent. They needed the lift that a final performance before that sellout crowd would provide. They needed the exhilaration of accomplishment one more time. They needed once again to so convincingly and so tenderly re-create the profound story of the last days of Jesus on earth.

They needed to know also that it was finished, for the first season at least. And they needed to know from the success of this night that it had been worth the sacrifice, that there would be another season next year—and the year after that....

So, when they gathered, later in the day, in the courtyard of the Church of St. Peter en Gallicantu there was an almost festive mood among them. They laughed, told jokes on one another, and remembered, alone and together, how they had come to be there at all.

The courtyard of St. Peter's had been turned into a small amphitheater. With the blessing and help of the parish priests, the courtyard became the scene once again of the suffering of Jesus the Nazarene, the telling of his message, and the search for understanding among men. It had been, as the press releases recalled, the first time in two thousand years that Jesus had been crucified again in Jerusalem.

The inspiration behind the Passion Play and the transformation of the courtyard came from the mind and heart of the same man whose devotion and vision had, in fact, brought them there in the first place: Francisco de Araujo.

Producer and director of the Jerusalem Passion Play, and so much more as we'll learn later, Araujo knew that the churchyard was *the* location for his production the moment he first set foot on the ancient steps leading up the side of Mount Zion and through the yard.

"After all," he remembers, "these are the steps that Jesus himself walked before his crucifixion, two thousand years ago."

Perhaps more compelling for Araujo and for all who come to the place is the dungeon buried deep beneath the church. It is said that it was there that Jesus was held captive during the night before they came to take him to the Cross. How desperately lonely he must have been that night! Not alone, for his Father was with him. But lonely.

The dungeon is a deep pit carved out of the rock. Its walls rise some ten feet before there is an opening ... to allow light in in the daytime and through which his captors could watch him by night. From this place there could have been no escape, no rescue.

There could be only the end that had been prophesied and for which he had prepared himself earlier that very night in the Garden of Gethsemane, where he prayed three times. How human he seemed then, knowing that he would die for the sins of the world but wondering whether there might be a way for him to remain among the living, on earth; to continue his ministry among his people. To somehow convince them, through other than a violent and degrading finish, that he *was* the son of their God.

But it was not to be, and he said, "My Father, if this cup cannot pass by without my drinking it, your will be done."

It is said, too, that the place on Mount Zion where the Church of St. Peter en Gallicantu now stands, the house of Caiaphas stood. Caiaphas, the high priest, before whom Jesus was brought to be interrogated and subjected to the fears of the then ruling establishment among Jews.

How touching, and important to a dramatist such as Francisco de Araujo, that this should also have been the place where the disciple Peter denied his Lord three times. So much, it seems, of crucial importance to the Passion took place on the very site selected by Araujo to re-create the crucifixion story.

None of this could fail to make an impression as I waited in the stands that day of the last performance in the premier season of the Jerusalem Passion Play. In fact, little of the story behind the Passion Play can fail to make an impression.

To Christians and Jews alike the Passion story has stirred the deepest emotions for nearly two thousand years. It has caused those who could call themselves Christians, after the death of Jesus, to realize the true meaning of love and to carry that message throughout the world as civilization spread. But the Passion story would also become a banner under which those same Christians would impose upon the Jews the most ghastly and repressive denials of human rights.

Haunted by the mystery of the story and the misfortunes heaped upon them since then (and somehow foretold in the prophecy of the Old Testament), Jews have spent centuries in fear and suspicion of Christians. It is only in relatively recent times that the real threat to the Jews has been assumed by the Arab world.

That Francisco de Araujo would dare to dream of bringing the Passion Play to the very location from which the centuries-old misunderstandings were born is startling enough. That he would bring it off successfully has been called by many a miracle. It has been seen by many others as God's will.

There was precious little time for Araujo to rest. Even then, visions of great words and music danced in his mind.

155

If it was divine intervention that made the Passion Play possible, then, too, it must have been divine guidance that brought about the creation of the Jewish state, the State of Israel, in 1948. This is said because without the State of Israel and the visionary leadership of the nation and the city of Jerusalem there would likely have been little to recommend Araujo's effort and not much of a place extant in which to attempt his production.

Whatever one's politics as the twentieth century races to a close, the fact is that the Israelis have created a democratic society in which the worship of all religions, and the exploration of even that which the Jews hold so mysterious and historically threatening, has been assured under modern law.

This devotion to those principles that we hold so dear in the United States came to me only after I had spent some time in Israel and with those who govern it.

It has been said by reporters stationed in Israel and by some practical politicians in Jerusalem that the Israelis will do just about anything to gather friends to their side. That may be true. It cannot be overstated that Israel is a nation surrounded on all sides but the Mediterranean Sea by hostile forces. Under such circumstances, one must gather friends wherever one can find them.

But, I suggest, there is another motivation for this forthright willingness to welcome all to their shores and society. That motivation comes from God. The same God who guided the Jews through so much travail before the appearance of Yeshua the Nazarene (I use his Hebrew name here for a reason), who sent his only son into the world so long ago and who sent other prophets (Muhammad, it is said) to report his word to whoever would listen.

How else can one explain the yearning over the centuries by the Jews to regain their homeland: the land of David, Abraham, and Isaac? How else

can one explain their dedication and devotion—once they had regained that land—to its restoration and flowering?

Was it simply, as some would have us agree, that they needed a place to retreat after the many abuses and persecutions of the centuries? Even those who carried the Christian message so widely throughout the world seemed to have forgotten the home of Jesus as a place to be preserved as it was when Jesus walked there. The followers of Muhammad carried their worship and locus to the east, to Mecca and Medina. Only the Jews would try, again and again, to return to his place.

I do not suggest here that we in the Christian world simply forgot where it had all begun. What we did do, apparently, was substitute other places for Jerusalem, in the belief that wherever we were he would be. And so he has been to those who have truly believed in his message and suffering. After all, the world of Jesus was not much larger than that which we now call the Middle East. And he did implore his followers to go forth with the message, wherever it might take them.

But only the Jews persisted in seeking ways to return, physically as well as spiritually. For their perseverance, the Christian world should be grateful to the people of David. Their return to Israel has directed our attention, perhaps as in no earlier period of modern history, to the place from whence we have come and the place where he served all of us.

To the Christian, the going forth into the world is the Great Commission. "Go, therefore, make disciples of all nations; baptize them in the name of the Father and of the Son and of the Holy Spirit, and teach them to observe all of the commands I gave you. And know that I am with you always; yes, to the end of time."

Lance Lambert, in his book *The Uniqueness of Israel,* reports an interesting commentary on the Jews returning to their homeland. According

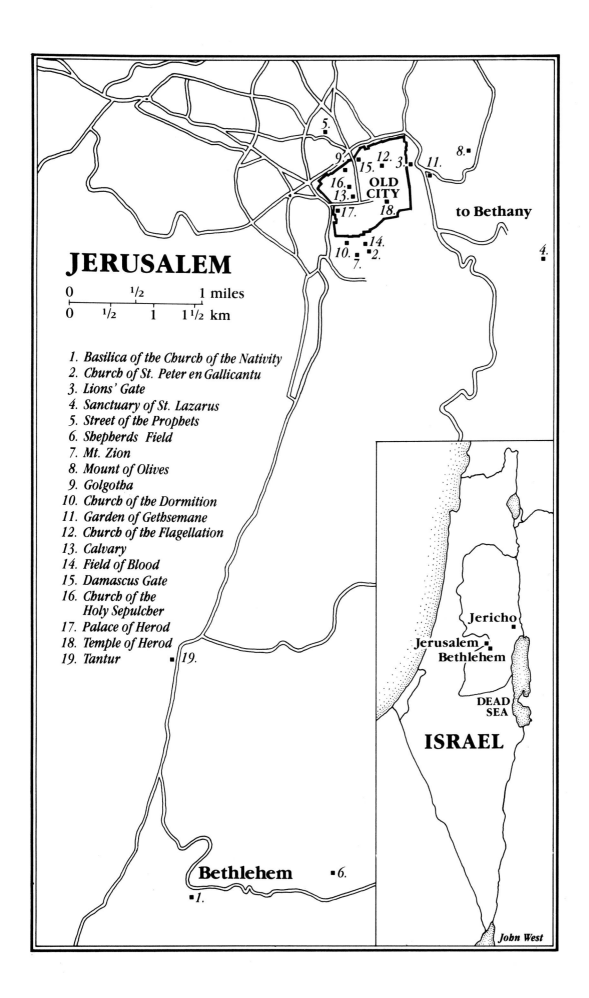

JERUSALEM

0   ½   1 miles
0   ½   1   1½ km

1. *Basilica of the Church of the Nativity*
2. *Church of St. Peter en Gallicantu*
3. *Lions' Gate*
4. *Sanctuary of St. Lazarus*
5. *Street of the Prophets*
6. *Shepherds Field*
7. *Mt. Zion*
8. *Mount of Olives*
9. *Golgotha*
10. *Church of the Dormition*
11. *Garden of Gethsemane*
12. *Church of the Flagellation*
13. *Calvary*
14. *Field of Blood*
15. *Damascus Gate*
16. *Church of the*
    Holy Sepulcher
17. *Palace of Herod*
18. *Temple of Herod*
19. *Tantur*

OLD CITY

to Bethany

Bethlehem

ISRAEL

Jericho

Jerusalem
Bethlehem

DEAD
SEA

John West

to Lambert, "There is a story told of Napoleon that he passed a crowded synagogue on the 9th Avenue and, arrested by the noise of obvious weeping and sorrow, he asked what it meant. He was told that they were weeping in the synagogue for their country and their sanctuary which had been destroyed some 1,800 years before. Napoleon, deeply moved, observed that 'A people which weeps and mourns for the loss of its homeland 1,800 years ago and does not forget—such a people will never be destroyed. Such a people can rest assured that its homeland will be returned to it.'"

As the Jews had dreamed, been possessed, of returning to their homeland someday, so Francisco de Araujo has dreamed, been possessed, of bringing the message of the Passion to great audiences almost from the time of his earliest years.

It has been said that Araujo is a genius. If this be so, and I believe it is, then his character and background should give evidence of his genius. It does not. And then again it does, if one understands genius to be a combination of spirit, quality, and the power to influence others for good.

A man of medium height and weight, with a mane of prematurely white hair that he refuses to brush, Araujo certainly looks the role of genius. And he speaks, communicates, with an animated eloquence that somehow defies argument. Above all, perhaps, he is the embodiment of the long-suffering artist, capable of unswerving devotion to an idea and ideal, in spite of the odds. With it all, Francisco de Araujo is capable of deep love of his fellow man and a disarming way of projecting good humor. No brooding recluse, he is able to laugh at himself and the world around him.

We met one brilliantly sunny day in Jerusalem, in his Hilton hotel room high above the city. The premier season of the Passion Play was at its midpoint.

I asked him about his career—when this dream, this passion of his, had begun.

"It has always been there," he said. "I can't remember when it wasn't there. There was always this fascination with the first century and with Bible stories, Old Testament stories.

"We were a very religious family. Dad brought the family around the altar and prayed every night and sang a song. We prayed before eating. He is a very, very religious man. He is a saint, an absolute saint. My Mom is, too.

"When I was a kid of six or seven I would act out Bible stories by myself. I would do a whole show, an entire Bible story by myself. I'd play all the parts, I'd produce it, write it, costume it, the whole business.

"I'd go out in the woods where I had fixed a little area where I could do these shows by myself. No people, just by myself."

Araujo was alone, too, in his desire to play the piano, to do something that seemed inconsistent with the work ethic of his father, the son of a fisherman from the Azores. One of seven children, Francisco could do little more than make-believe at playing the piano on the windowsill during his first ten years. Only when the family arrived early in church, at Francisco's urging, did he have a chance to practice on a real piano.

At age twelve, while still in grade school, the precocious youngster won a debating contest on the evils of liquor. For his convincing arguments in favor of temperance he won the twenty-five-dollar first prize. With the money he bought his first piano.

Araujo remembers that time and what happened as a result very well indeed.

"When that thing came rolling into the house, I came rolling with it. It was wonderful to have a piano. It was out of tune. You couldn't tell one note from the other. But I had a piano at last.

"There was no way I could study. Dad was working at two jobs. He had seven kids to support. In addition to running his little farm, he worked in the village factory making stoves. He worked on those great big ovens with the enamelwork.

"One day he said to me, 'I can give you a dollar a week. If you can find a piano teacher for a dollar a week, you can have piano lessons.' I was thrilled. I searched out a piano teacher for a dollar a week and I started piano lessons. You can imagine the kind of teaching I had for a dollar a week. It was the local jazz guy. He would say, 'This is A, this C, now get with it.' My lesson paid for one more dollar's worth of scotch for that night. The temperance kid was paying for it.

"I must have progressed quickly because I came to the attention of Ada Renzi, a very serious musician who offered me a scholarship. She had studied with world-famous musicians. Suddenly she opened the page and I was really into the world of music.

"She told me about her teacher, Virginia-Gene Rittenhouse, the world-famous violinist, concert pianist, and composer. From what I heard of Virginia-Gene, she might as well have been God to me.

"After two years I began to blossom. But I felt so inadequate because I had started so late.

"I didn't hear a concert until I was seventeen. I fell to pieces when I first heard it. In an all-Beethoven Concert, I heard the Emperor Concerto, the Seventh Symphony, and the Choral Fantasy for piano, chorus, and orchestra, which can you believe, in a command performance, I recently conducted for President Sadat.

"Until that time the only concert music I knew was the music I would hear on the radio, and I would say to myself, what is that? What instruments are those? It was such a strange thing to hear great music. It would do something inside me that I couldn't explain.

"When I graduated from high school, I didn't know what to do next.

"I didn't feel that I could pursue mu-

sic as a career. I didn't have that kind of background. I had one year of piano with a jazz pianist and two years of piano with Mrs. Renzi. I was ready for college but certainly not ready for conservatory.

"One day during a lesson my teacher said, 'I think you ought to audition for Virginia-Gene.' I froze. How could I? To me, it would be like standing before God.

"Finally I wrote to Virginia-Gene to ask if there was any way that I could play for her, to see if she thought I might have the talent to become a musician. Immediately a letter came saying she would hear me play.

"Walking into her house was like walking into the home of a truly great composer. Two Steinway pianos, paintings, marvelous curtains, drapes, chandeliers. I played the first movement of a Beethoven sonata. It must have been just awful!

"But after hearing me play she said, 'I detect all of the fire, energy, and enthusiasm needed, but of course you have a long way to go. I accept you as a pupil.' Immediately, she offered me a scholarship.

"From that day there developed the greatest possible relationship between student and teacher. She was the most powerful influence of my life. She is probably my dearest friend. If it hadn't been for her I would have died—emotionally, spiritually, everything. I studied with her through my college years at Atlantic Union College in Massachusetts."

Araujo's big break came while he was in the Master program at Boston University's School of Fine Arts, although he didn't see it that way when it first appeared. He received an invitation to go to Japan to organize a music program for a mission college there.

"The kids at the school had never had music. I was not only in charge of four years of junior school and four years of senior school, but also four years of college. When I saw the first little girl with bangs, I knew I would see her all the way through college.

"There were no music books. I had to prepare everything. There were only four old pianos of 1903 vintage. Still, I told the student body, 'We are going to see to it that everyone who wishes will be able to study piano. Let's see the hands of those who wish to study.' The entire student body raised their hands.

"One day an American came to speak at chapel. I never went to chapel because it was always in official Japanese, which is so different from the student Japanese I knew that I wouldn't have understood it anyhow. But at the urging of my students I went to hear the American preacher.

"I'd been so crazy busy that I knew nothing about Japan. I had just jumped in with all fours and started doing what I thought had to be done, teaching music, nothing else.

"Then the preacher began talking about Japan. He told us that there were well over one hundred million people living in Japan and it was no larger than the state of California.

"I nearly died. I had no idea.

"Then he said, 'Do you know how many Christians there are in this country of one hundred and twenty million?' O Lord, I asked, let it be at least ten million.

"The preacher said, 'Do you know that there are fewer than 100,000 Christians in all of this country?'

"In my great anxiety to do what I thought that I had to do, I had ignored all of this.

"I ran to my home, slammed the door behind me and said, 'Lord, why did you send me here? What on earth—what mistake have you made? Why am I here teaching kids piano? What has this got to do with what we have to do here?' I cried. I felt he should have sent Billy Graham.

"Well, something came out of that despair and I realized that I wasn't going to be excused. God wasn't going to excuse me from what I had to do. From that moment, I determined that I was going to create a choral society in Japan that would present through music all the great themes of Christianity. It became an obsession with me.

"We organized a choral society and, in one year, had its debut in Tokyo.

"The first concert was an extraordinary thing. I did all of the publicity myself. I put up posters—everything. I conducted and I was even the piano soloist in the concert. There was standing room only. These were kids from rice paddies who had never been on a stage in their lives. But they sang like angels—all religious music. The critics raved and a new idea had been launched.

"One miracle happened after another, because our work together had instilled the kids with faith. Their faith grew more than mine—my faith grew because they forced it to grow. I had planted the seed and it grew like an oak.

"Things snowballed until we were doing our concerts in the new opera house in Tokyo. Imagine, Bernstein and Francisco de Araujo and his Choral Arts Society, together, in Japan.

"After that, I decided we were ready. We would tour all over Japan and tell, through music, the story and the message of Jesus.

"As I went from place to place the Communist movement was sure that I was on the CIA payroll. But in reality I was just my own Peace Corps.

"Visiting Nagoya State University one day, I suggested to the student leaders, 'I've got a choral group coming into the city. You've got an orchestra. We'll do a joint concert. I'll train your orchestra.' I knew that this university didn't have a music department and that the kids did their own thing. I told them that I'd come and work with them all summer. We would put it together with my chorus and I would play the Beethoven Choral Fantasy with the orchestra and the chorus. I told them I would even do the piano part. They said, 'Oh, this is a great idea!'

"It was incredible. No sooner had I

arrived than the Communists moved in. They threatened a riot in front of my concert. They threatened to kill me. The night before the opening, they demanded that we cancel the concert. It was an enormous test of faith, of Communism versus Christianity.

"I said that I wanted to talk to the orchestra. So I brought my choir right in front of them in the rehearsal room. The head of the opposition was sitting in the back and I didn't even know it. We sang the 'Lord's Prayer' of Leroy Robertson, the Mormon composer. In the darkened hall, a hush fell over the orchestra; the acoustics lent itself to a beautiful rendition. It seemed as if angels sang with us.

"The professor in charge of the orchestra stood up and said, 'Oh, we must apologize, this is so beautiful. Of course we must do the concert.' The concert went on, but only after I had agreed to hold a public debate on Christianity versus Communism after the concert. During the four years of its performance, it was estimated later that, in concert and on television, some forty million heard our Choral Arts Society in Japan.

"Next the group was invited on a concert tour of the United States. They sang in six languages. In ninety days we made two hundred appearances—from the United Nations to the White House to Town Hall in New York. They became the darlings of America.

"The last concert was in Portland, Oregon. We were all made honorary citizens. There we did a concert for fifteen thousand people. After the concert we boarded the bus that would take us to the airport. Hundreds of people were there to say goodbye.

"Suddenly I realized the job was finished. All of this after that frustrating moment on my knees when I said to the Lord, O.K., you don't excuse me but I expect something extraordinary. That's how I got into conducting."

On the basis of the success of the Japan years, Araujo was accepted as a

doctoral student at the Peabody Conservatory in Baltimore, Maryland. He returned to Washington and commuted to Peabody. He also started to organize various choral groups. He founded the National Choral Society and the Alexandria Choral Society for the city of Alexandria, Virginia. His return to Washington would set him on a collision course with the Jerusalem Passion Play.

Although he has never had the time to complete the paperwork for his doctorate—his career got in the way—Araujo conducted his three required recitals in an unusual way. Doctoral recitals are performed in residence at the conservatory. In Araujo's case, unusual permission was granted. His recitals were given as open concerts at Carnegie Hall in New York, and in Washington, D.C., at both J.F.K. Concert Hall and D.A.R. Constitution Hall.

"After the last recital Paul Hume of the Washington *Post* wrote that at one point in the program the audience burst into well-deserved applause. Wrote Paul Hume, 'It will be interesting to see what Araujo does, what path he takes.'

"A year or so later, I called Paul Hume to ask his advice about my idea to perform Bach's *St. Matthew Passion* as a kind of ancient morality play. He didn't particularly like the idea and reminded me that several other groups were going to do the traditional performance in the city.

Director Araujo and his troupe rehearsed constantly to achieve the power of Jesus' passion; here with Greg Strom.

"Hume cautioned me, 'Why don't you do something different?'"

Just about this time, Church Women United of Greater Washington contacted Araujo and asked him to do a special concert for Easter. He suggested that Bach's *St. Matthew Passion* be performed as a theater piece in costume like an opera. They loved the idea.

Opening night was a sellout. The Washington *Star* critic captioned his headline "Bach Passion Highlight of the Easter Season. If you want to see the characters of the Passion leap out at you, go and see Araujo's production. Araujo's production deserves to be heard everywhere."

There was still no word from Paul Hume at the *Post*. The second performance was concluded and still not a word from Paul Hume.

As it turned out, he had been there opening night. That night, explained Araujo, they did have a couple of technical problems. After the last rehearsal the lighting director unknowingly changed some stagelights in a way that produced glare right into the eyes of the woodwind section. As he was conducting they could not see him. So some of the important entrances were late.

"After the second performance we heard that there was going to be a review the next morning in the Washington *Post*. While I was driving our soprano to her hotel after the show she said, 'Why don't we stop and get the review?'

"It was the most awful moment of my life. Paul Hume slaughtered me.

"He wrote, 'Murder in the cathedral ... this cannot be tolerated. It's like slashing the great da Vinci with a knife.' He wanted to run me out of town. He detected that the baritone had a cold and he blamed that on me. I thought, 'If you can bear to hear the truth be spoken and twisted by knaves to make a trap for fools and watch the things you gave your life for broken ...' He spared nothing. It was the disaster of disasters. I boast of having

the worst review in history of criticism. But justice prevailed. One review played against the other. It created a sensation in Washington.

"Some of the musicians in the orchestra called Paul Hume; everyone called Paul Hume. 'Hume,' they asked, 'do you understand what Araujo was trying to do? He is bringing Bach's monumental score to the masses....' But, he stayed by his guns. To all of us in the company, it was an assassination! Total and complete. It was my first bad review.

"I had one more performance to go. It was sold out, too. How would I face the next morning?

"The next day I thought, if you believe in what you are doing, go ahead and do it anyhow. When I walked into the costume room, someone had taken words from Hume's review and printed them on a streamer right across the costume room. It read THIS MUST NOT BE TOLERATED! It broke the ice. The entire troupe came around and we hugged and kissed one another.

"The big test came when I walked onto the stage. It was such an awkward moment. It was like a death in the family.

"Since the play was in a cathedral, we had the Dean of the cathedral walk in first. It was like a processional. As I walked in, the whole audience stood.

"I knew then that I would have to pursue my Passion Play idea with my own passion. That review. If I had gotten only the rave review, I probably would not have pursued it. It would not have become a passion. But because of the bad review, I had to prove somehow that my approach to the Passion was not wrong.

"During that performance I remember conducting the last chorus as they sang 'Around Thy Tomb Sit We Weeping.' I had turned the cathedral into the tomb. We threw light from outside against the stained glass and turned the church into a spectacle of color. It made it appear that we were *all* sitting in the tomb while the chorus sang. When I turned to look at Jesus lying on

Arabs, Israelis, Americans. Young, not so young, and very young, they gathered with pride to tell the Bible story of Jesus.

the bier, I saw that the audience was sobbing. It was a moving experience.

"Somehow Paul Hume had come away with the wrong impression about what I was trying to do with the Passion story. He was looking at the Passion in a totally different way than I was. He didn't understand what I was trying to do. I was trying to bring Bach to the masses in a way that would be a touching, personal experience.

"I couldn't let it rest. It was an injustice, not to me, but to the Passion. One can get over a bad review, but in this case the Passion had been assailed, in my estimation."

Five years later, Araujo made his first trip to the Holy Land.

He made the trip when he was asked to conduct a concert for Egyptian President Anwar el-Sadat. Though fraught with difficulties, the concert was a resounding success.

During that trip Araujo was overcome with emotion as he sat by himself in the sacred shrines of Bethlehem and Jerusalem. He was close to his Lord at last. Araujo would realize only after he had returned home to Washington that the desire to perform the Passion Play in Jerusalem itself had been born. The year was 1980.

After Araujo was home again in Washington, the friend who had promoted the Egyptian tour called and said that he had another group getting ready for a Holy Land tour. He asked if Araujo would go with them, more as a guide than anything else. The Bible-conscious conductor answered that he would go, but only on the condition that he would remain behind in Jerusalem.

"My friend," Araujo said. "I am going to do the Passion Play in Jerusalem! Would you like to sponsor it?"

Araujo's friend liked the idea. But after many months of searching he was not able to generate the financing required to support the production. In fact, as Araujo recalls, his talent and time and energy became hostage to the sometimes unscrupulous persons who finance creative endeavors. Raising money for any large theatrical or motion picture production is not easy. The objectives of those with the money are often not the same as those of the creative persons. How much more difficult it was when the creative idea was a Passion Play in Jerusalem, the very site of an explosive two-thousand-year-old misunderstanding!

The supercharged director needed much more than money. He needed the backing of an inspired Christian who would be prepared, if necessary, to risk everything to support Araujo's commitment to expurgate the Passion story as it has been presented by other Christian groups for centuries. He knew that unless the so-called anti-Semitism of the Passion was removed from his production it could never be presented in Israel, and rightly so as far as he was concerned.

Araujo was determined to present the Passion story in a spirit of reconciliation between Christians and Jews. His reading of the Bible places the blame for the crucifixion on all of us, not on the Jews. He needed a backer who shared this interpretation of the Bible. More importantly, perhaps, Araujo needed a backer who would share his belief that when Jesus said from the Cross, "Father, forgive them, for they know not what they do," he meant to forgive all people, including the Jews.

In the end, that backer would appear to Araujo in the person of Frank Parsons, a lawyer, tour operator, and onetime candidate for mayor of Birmingham, Alabama. He is a devoted Christian layman and parishioner at the McElwain Baptist Church, in Birmingham. Parsons first heard of Araujo's Passion Play almost by accident. Or was it providence?

Through the year 1980, Araujo had continued his struggle to bring the Passion Play into being, but without success. The group with whom he was working still could not raise the money. Their one, last chance would come, they believed, at the 1981 Convention of Religious Broadcasters. An annual affair held in Washington, the convention is attended by travel agents and tour operators looking to promote their services to the Holy Land. If the Passion Play company could not attract investment from this group, plans for mounting the Play in 1981 would have to be abandoned for another year, perhaps forever. Araujo just could not go on any longer without compensation for his effort. The

personal financial strain was becoming unbearable.

Araujo went to the convention filled with hope, but not much else. The group with whom he had originally developed the project continued to play its game with his emotions and his devotion to the project. They knew, he remembers, that they could do whatever they wished with him, because they knew he wanted the Passion Play perhaps more than anything else in his life.

The convention was about over, with no results. No investor had been found to save the project. It had been an exhausting time, filled with everything from fruitless discussions with some who said they might be interested to wandering from booth to booth dropping off brochures about the play.

Just as Araujo was about to leave, a young man walked up to the dejected director and said, "Mr. Araujo, my boss would like to speak to you about the Passion Play."

Araujo recognized the fellow as Jim Parrish, the sales director from the booth of Echols Tours, where he had dropped off a clutch of brochures earlier in the day.

Tired, frustrated, and suspecting yet another come-on, Araujo told the young man he was not interested. He was going home. But the man persisted, and Araujo agreed to pass by and meet Frank Parsons at the Echols booth on the way out of the building.

Believing he had nothing to lose, Araujo poured out the entire desperate history of the Passion Play and its financial plight in their first meeting. What Araujo could not have known then was that Frank Parsons was prepared to go all the way to acquire the rights to the Play. It was the opportunity he had been looking for, which would allow him to combine a deep belief in the Christian message with his ever-present desire to expand his tour operation to the Holy Land. Parsons didn't know much about show business at that moment. Nor did he know that it would ultimately cost him over one million dollars to present the premier season of the Play in Jerusalem. In the months that followed he would learn much and give more.

Says Araujo about the step that Frank Parsons took that day: "For me, it was like being in the pit and being picked up by one man, and that was Frank Parsons."

From that day forward, Frank Parsons gave to the man with the obsession with the Passion story what he needed most: the independence to pursue his dream and to concentrate on the creative effort that would make the dream a reality.

Parsons would be required to make many sacrifices to preserve Araujo's creative independence. He would mortgage his business, cajole his friends to invest, alienate a score of creditors, and cause some to question his motives. But he, like the man he was supporting, would persevere and in the end share the triumph of that first season's closing performance on Mount Zion itself. If Frank Parsons had been seeking a way to serve his Lord through business, he had found it.

In order to understand the magnitude of the challenge that faced Francisco de Araujo and his sponsor, Frank Parsons, one needs to appreciate the history of Judeo-Christian relations since the crucifixion, as well as the history of the Passion Play since the seventeenth century. From this history one can see more clearly why the people of Israel might not have been too enamored of the idea to re-create the crucifixion in Jerusalem.

For purposes of this review, I have chosen to rely most on the profound study by Father Jean Paul Lichtenberg, who, until his death, in Strasbourg on Palm Sunday in 1972, had been an adviser to the Roman Catholic archbishop there and an associate of the Ecumenical Theological Research Fraternity, in Israel. Brought to my attention by the Reverend Dr. Wesley

Brown, chairman of the Fraternity, the study is "a spiritual Testament which seeks a new relationship between Christians and Jews by drawing the proper lessons from the sad history of their encounters in the past."

Wes Brown is director of Special Studies at the Ecumenical Institute for Advanced Theological Studies at Tantur, an intellectual oasis on the main road between Jerusalem and Bethlehem. Dr. Brown is an intense, soft-spoken man whose devotion to the biblical message of love is exceptional. The helping hand that he and his family extended to Araujo and to me was strong and kind. His spirit and personality have endeared Dr. Brown to Jerusalem's community leaders.

Writing about the Jerusalem Passion Play, in his regular column of commentary in the Jerusalem *Post,* and in his musings with me, Dr. Brown seems to suggest that the Play is at least a positive new addition to Father Lichtenberg's study *From the First to the Last of the Just.* As an optimist, I suggest the impact of the Play on Judeo-Christian relations may become more significant than even Wes Brown can foretell.

The title of Father Lichtenberg's study derives from the novel by André Schwarz-Bart *The Last of the Just,* which was awarded the Goncourt Prize in 1959. To summarize the poignant and often angry thrust of the young French Jew's novel, Lichtenberg chose the following passage. It is a dialogue between Ernie Levy, the hero of the piece, and his fiancée, Golda, who wears the Star of David.

"Oh, Ernie," Golda said, "you know them. Tell me why, why do the Christians hate us the way they do? They seem so nice when I can look at them without my Star."

Ernie put his arms around her shoulders solemnly.

"It's very mysterious," he murmured in Yiddish. "They don't know exactly why themselves. I've been in their churches and I've read their gospel. Do you know who the Christ was? A simple Jew like your father. A kind of Hassid [a devout man]."

Golda smiled gently. "You're kidding me."

"No, no, believe me, and I'll bet they'd have got along fine, the two of them, because he was really a good Jew, you know, sort of like a Baal Shem Tov [founder of the Hassidic movement]—a merciful man, and gentle. The Christians say they love him, but I think they hate him without knowing it. So they take the cross by the other end and make a sword out of it and strike us with it! You understand, Golda," he cried suddenly, strangely excited, "they take the cross and turn it around, they turn it around, my God. . . ."

[Golda tries to calm her friend Ernie, but he continues, obstinately:]

"Poor Jesus, if he came back to earth and saw that the pagans had made a sword out of him and used it against his sisters and brothers, he'd be sad, he'd grieve forever. And maybe he does see it. They say that some of the Just Men remain outside the gates of Paradise, that they don't want to forget humanity, that they, too, await the Messiah. Yes, maybe he does see it. Who knows? You understand, Goldeleh, he was a little old-fashioned Jew, a real Just Man, you know, no more nor less than . . . all our Just Men."

There we have it. The consternation, sadness, and fear of so many Ernie Levys throughout history who have been held to account for the death of Jesus at the hands of Pontius Pilate and the local Jewish establishment of the day.

Father Lichtenberg admits to a certain difficulty in tracing the "tangled web of Christian anti-Judaism and anti-Semitism" even among theological historians. And, he suggests, the Jews have not been entirely without fault in causing the rift. But the overwhelming body of evidence seems to identify Christians as the aggressors most of the time.

Lichtenberg traces the history of Judeo-Christian relations through five major periods: from the Crucifixion to the ascent to the throne of Emperor Constantine (in 313); from the fourth century to the period of the Crusades; from the Crusades to the end of the Middle Ages and the beginning of the Renaissance; from the Renaissance to the end of the eighteenth century, which marks the periods of Jewish emancipation; and finally from the nineteenth century to the twentieth century, which ushers in the appearance of modern anti-Semitism.

Recognizing the Jewishness of Jesus, the French priest writes that opposition to the Judeo-Christians of the "sect" of Jesus the Nazarene began in the course of the development, within Judaism itself, of the Christian community of Jewish origin. He continues: "Tension in the relations between Jews and Christians began with the martyrdom of Stephen and the departure of Paul—the former Pharisee turned Christian—on a mission around the Mediterranean basin. The representatives of Palestinian Judaism fought against and persecuted those who became converted to the 'Path' of Jesus the Galilean, because to them this was heterodoxy."

More concerned with spreading the Good News than becoming embroiled in the political struggle their Jewish compatriots were then pursuing with the Roman rulers of Palestine, the Christians were seen as traitors. "In disassociating itself from the national cause, the 'sect' of the Nazarene cut its ties with Judaism to turn towards new shores." Christians would look back only in anger for the next nineteen centuries.

The Jews who remained to battle the Romans for their homeland were driven from the city of Jerusalem, and the Temple was turned into a sanctuary of Zeus and of Hadrian. Jews *and* Christians were dispersed into Transjordan and Syria to resume their internecine struggle. The idea that the Jews had been dispersed because of their rejection of Jesus as the son of God began to grow among Christians.

There followed three centuries of "progressive alienation" during which time the Christians were persecuted by Romans and Jews alike; the latter enjoying relative peace and legal status while Christianity remained illegal.

An "incredible turnabout" came in 312 with the victory of Constantine over Maxentius. The pagan empire became *Holy* Roman and Christian almost overnight—in the historical sense, anyway.

Jews, who had enjoyed the right of full Roman citizenship, were returned to a state of "institutional inferiority." Under Constantinian Christianity, the impact of the Tertullian polemic "Adversus Judaeos" was felt. It went "all the way from completely religious argumentation, as in the works of St. Augustine, to the manifestations of a sort of anti-Jewish hate bordering on anti-Semitism."

It is in those writings that it was presented for the first time as fact that the Jews were collectively responsible for the death of Jesus; that the entire history of Israel was basically a long series of transgressions. It was here that the Christian apologists first set forth the idea that God cast out the Jews as divine punishment. "Among the triumphalist hymns of this epoch, anti-Jewish song was to have its place, in particular in the liturgy of Good Friday." Then came the Crusades.

For the Jews now living in Europe, the period of the Crusades would be their worst—until the Holocaust. Father Lichtenberg states strongly that "The period of the Crusades impaired forever the relations between Christians and Jews living in the Western world."

In the year 1009, word spread through Europe that the Muslims had destroyed the Church of the Holy Sepulcher in Jerusalem. The Caliph of Cairo had been incited to this terrible deed by the Jews, the tale went on to say. By the time Pope Urban II got around to launching the First Crusade, in 1096, the flames of anti-Semitism and hatred for the Jewish "killers of Christ" had been fanned to white heat. The Ishmaelites (Muslims), who had by now occupied the holy places as the Jews scurried for cover, became one with the Jews. Throughout France and Germany, on their way to smite the infidel, the Crusaders fell upon the Jews with a vengeance.

There were Christian leaders who tried to protect the Jews from the gruesome excesses of the uninformed and misguided. But the attempt of some civil or religious authorities, such as Bishop Cosmas of Prague, to restrain this "unleashing of passions was more often than not fruitless."

One of those men is remembered in a Jewish chronicle of the Second Crusade for his vigorous defense of the people of Israel. About this man, the writer states: "The Lord hearkened to our pleadings and turned towards us in His great pity, sending us ... after this monster [the German monk Rudolph] another worthy monk, one of the greatest and most reputable among the monks, one who knew and understood their Law. His name was Bernard ... of the city of Clairvaux in France. He too preached in accordance with their custom and said: 'It is a good thing to want to go and fight against the Ishmaelites. Nevertheless, whosoever lays a hand upon a Jew to take his life commits a sin as enormous as though he laid his hand upon the person of Jesus himself. . . .' If the Creator had not sent this monk, no vestige of Israel would have been left."

As the Middle Ages came to a close, the Jews were expelled from England, from France, from Portugal, and from Spain, an event considered by most scholars "a veritable catastrophe in Jewish history," since it wrote finis to Spanish Jewry in the West. Poland became an asylum of Judaism. Retiring there unto themselves, they established a medieval ghetto. To escape the pressures of the outside, or non-Jewish, world and to provide spiritual and temporal haven, they retreated into themselves.

"The ghetto was not a question merely of an institution, but also a state of mind. For centuries, Jews had been able to take up arms and defend themselves when necessary. As a consequence of the persecutions and the humiliations of the second part of the Middle Ages, Ashkenazi (or central European) Judaism gradually adopted a more passive attitude in the face of persecution and harassment, seeking in the ghetto a feeling of security and liberty." It was a movement and change of mentality for which the Jews would be sorrowful centuries later, and to which they would react violently after the Second World War.

If the Renaissance did not completely emancipate the Jews in Europe, it did provide the environment of tolerance for new ideas and renewal of the human spirit that set the stage for emancipation. By the second half of the eighteenth century, racked as the Western world was then by successive revolutions, the Jews, "previously relegated to the margin of society, were integrated progressively in the countries in which they lived." This included, of course, the United States, where emancipation was "fundamental from the inception of the American constitution."

Meanwhile, in Europe, the French, through the "generous ideas of Montesquieu and the Abbé Grégoire" accorded to the Jews the same rights as all other citizens. The process was repeated in Germany, England, Austria, and Hungary through the end of the nineteenth century. It brought with it the flowering of Jewish thought and creative expression.

Alas, the granting of rights and the assimilation into their societies did not assuage those in whom the fires of animosity still burned. The Jews, these persons said, were not Germans. They were not French. They were something else, something of another world. Besides, they appeared to be too much involved with the economics of those societies. German ethnological philosophy and science, through a man named Schlozer, invented the word Semite in 1781. It was followed quickly by the word anti-Semitism. Out of jealousy, fear, or a perverse reading of the Scriptures, there were those who would cause, by the time of the Weimar Republic, in Germany, the Jews to again fear for their very lives.

Growing to power out of that 1933 economic crisis in Germany, Adolf Hitler set in motion the most fearful and murderous wave of anti-Semitism in history. But this was a *new* form of anti-Semitism. It was called "neopagan racist anti-Semitism."

Whatever its label, it appears to have developed because "Christian establishment anti-Semitism, rationalist anti-Semitism, and the passions of Christian resentment had sensitized and prepared the way to Nazi propaganda to a degree previously unknown." The new anti-Semitism had other roots, as well. "The doctrine of the *Herrenvolk*, propagated by the likes of Goebbels and Rosenberg, the Nazi party theoreticians, was in no way inspired by the ideas of the Apologists and the Fathers of the Church, but by those of the pseudo-scholars who introduced the myth of the two races—Aryan and Semitic—on the basis of which Nietzsche was able, in part, to elaborate the philosophy of the will for power."

Nazi doctrine was anti-Jewish. It was also anti-Christ, in the sense that Christians should have understood Christ. As with other repressive sociopolitical movements of the twentieth century, the leaders of Nazi Germany bothered very little to justify their ghastly actions as providential. Why should they? They were totally Godless.

This does not imply an excuse for what happened to the Jews throughout Nazi-dominated Christian Europe.

There is none. Still, it is probably going too far to suggest, as some have, that the Holocaust was the result of some grand Christian conspiracy. Rather, this most devastating scourge of our fellow men, women, and children was more likely a conspiracy of silence; a shameful refusal by most Christians to admit and speak out in support of the teachings of both the Old and the New covenants during that time of global crisis.

Seen against this background of historical anti-Semitism, one can more readily understand how the portrayal of the last days of Jesus through passion plays has perpetuated anti-Semitism. Lacking any offsetting guidance, well-meaning Christians have harped upon the deicide aspect of the Passion, rejected the facts of scripture, and denied the message of love and forgiveness contained in the Gospels.

The most celebrated Passion Play, until Francisco de Araujo came to Jerusalem, has been the one staged every ten years since 1634 in the Bavarian village of Oberammergau. Praying to the Lord for deliverance from a plague that ravaged the village in 1632, the village elders vowed to "keep the tragedy of the Passion every ten years" if they were delivered. When no deaths occurred for two years, the good people of the village met their obligation.

Because it became ever more elaborate a production with every decade, because it attracted the attention of Christians throughout the Western world, and finally because it is in the South of Germany, the Oberammergau Passion Play has been the target for years of those who seek to detoxify passion plays.

This effort has been led by the Anti-Defamation League of B'nai B'rith with the help of other interfaith and Jewish organizations such as the American Jewish Committee. Through consultation with the village elders of Oberammergau, Anti-Defamation League executives and Christian scholars have succeeded in gradually correcting many of the errors in the play script and production "that fly in the face of religious and historical truth."

To support its case for change in approach to the Passion story, the Anti-Defamation League cites proclamations made by the Second Vatican Council, the World Council of Churches, and the House of Bishops of the Episcopal Church. The Roman Church, in repudiating anti-Semitism, has called upon its members to foster love for the Jews as the people of Jesus, Mary, Peter, and Paul. Declaring anti-Semitism "a sin against God and man," Vatican Council II admonished the Catholic Church to denounce this ancient sin. Perhaps most pointedly, the Episcopalians state that "the charge of deicide against the Jews is a tragic misunderstanding of the inner significance of the crucifixion."

The Anti-Defamation League has published "Guidelines for the *Oberammergau Passionsspiel* and other Passion Plays." The guidelines and commentary which accompany them were prepared by Dr. Leonard Swidler, Professor of Catholic Thought and Interreligious Dialogue at Temple University. It is significant that Dr. Swidler reflects that his guidelines are "not those of Christians whose sole concern is the sensitivities of Jews." More important, Swidler suggests, is a concern that those Christians who attend Passion Play performances "should comprehend their own scriptures sufficiently to derive spiritual profit from them, and not depend in any sense on feelings of hostility for the furtherance of their religion."

Stating, quite correctly I think, that the Gospels are "transcendent works of faith and human genius," Swidler nonetheless recognizes that a drama based upon the Gospels gives the appearance "of being history when they are not history, but only based on history and set in history." Again correctly, Swidler observes that the Gospels are "closer to the dramatic medium than to the historical." Finally, he suggests, the Gospels "must be presented for what they are, dramatic writing that hopes to foster faith."

Because they *are* revealing and instructive to Christians and Jews alike (and it is hoped that ever greater numbers of Jewish people will also avail themselves of the Passion Play experience), Dr. Swidler's guidelines are presented here in their entirety:

1. The play should avoid creating the "impression that most Jews of Jesus' day willed his death, failing to show that the secrecy surrounding much of Jesus' trial was motivated by the large following he had in Jerusalem." The vast majority of the eight million Jews then living had never heard of Jesus, much less rejected him. The crowd scene before Pilate should clearly and correctly reflect the fact that some in the crowd supported Jesus and that the rest were manipulated by his opponents, as is made clear in the Gospels.

2. The play should avoid depicting "Pilate—whom history and the Gospels have shown to have been a ruthless tyrant, a coward and a perverter of justice—as an innocent and kindly bystander, involved against his will in the persecution of Jesus." Only the Roman ruler could condemn someone to death. Roman soldiers executed Jesus in the specifically Roman manner, crucifixion. The sign Pilate had placed on Jesus' cross—"Jesus of Nazareth, King of the Jews"—shows pointedly that Pilate had Jesus executed as an insurrectionist. To portray Pilate as noble is to make "the Jews" the enemies of Jesus and "the Romans" his friends—a perversion of history and a stimulus to anti-Semitism.

3. The play should not speak of the "old" testament or covenant. To do so is unhistorical and un-Jesus-like. In the Hebrew Bible, which was the only Bible Jesus knew, there are several succeeding covenants. Each added to but did not replace the preceding ones, as is true of Jesus' "new" covenant. Christians may speak of "earlier" covenants, but never of an "old," outmoded covenant. Perhaps it is most precise to speak of one covenant, often stated anew in different times and circumstances.

4. The play should not give exclusively to enemies of Jesus recognizably Hebrew Bible names, such as Moses, Joshua, Ezekiel, and it should avoid recognizably "New Testament" names, such as John, James, Matthew. To do otherwise subtly and unwarrantedly establishes an opposition between the "Old" Testament and the "New," between "Jews" and "Christians."

5. The play should not give the impression that most of Jesus' opponents were Pharisees, or that all Pharisees opposed Jesus. (Nicodemus, for example, was a Pharisee and a follower of Jesus.) Nor should there be any "rabbis" among his opponents. At that time, "rabbi," which means "my teacher," was merely a form of address; it was, in fact, the way in which Jesus was addressed by his disciples.

It is false to set up an opposition between Jesus/Christianity and Pharisees, as such. Bearing in mind that Phariseeism is the spiritual ancestor of rabbinic and present-day Judaism, "it must be emphasized that Pharisaic doctrine is not opposed to that of Christianity ... the Pharisees and first Christians were in certain respects quite close to one another" (French Catholic Bishops' Committee for Relations with Jews).

6. The play must not "conceal the fact that Jesus is a Jew and that his apostles and friends as well as his enemies in the drama are Jews." Jesus and his followers were Jews; and they, doubtless, looked, spoke, and acted like other Jews. His name was not Jesus Christ, which is Greek; it was Yeshua of Nazareth, which is Semitic. He was addressed as "rabbi,"

and passion plays should do likewise. In short, Jesus and his followers should look and act like the Jews they were, and his opponents should not be cast as ugly stereotypes of Jews.

7. The play must not depict Jesus as opposed to the Law (Torah). Because Jesus was not a Christian but an observant Jew, he "carried out" (Matthew, 5:17ff.) the Law and taught his disciples to do the same. Nor must the Law, which Jesus so loved that he would not do away with "one jot or tittle" of it, be distorted in any way that would make it appear less than the great Law of love, which Jesus and other Jews before him summed up by quoting Deuteronomy, 6:5, and Leviticus, 19:18, as love of God and neighbor.

8. In summary: Passion plays should portray the events leading to the death of Jesus as a struggle among Jews, chief among them being Jesus. The struggle was about the best way to be Jewish; about how to live according to God's teaching—the Law (Torah).

The play should not leave us with thoughts of suspicion or feelings of disdain for Jesus' people, the Jews, of whom he was one. Rather, it should make us Gentile Christians grateful that we have been led to the one true God and to God's teaching (Torah) through the Jew, Jesus, the Christ for us.

By being faithful to religious and historical fact, the passion play should move us away from the error and evil of anti-Semitism. It should help foster in us love for the people of Jesus. And it should bring us to a more profound understanding and acceptance of the truth that, as is written in John, 4:22, our "salvation is from the Jews."

Francisco de Araujo was not consciously aware of the Guidelines for Passion Plays as he set out to realize his dream. But he knew what he believed. The Jews were not alone re-

There was no room for even a whisker to be out of place as they set out each night to tell the Passion story.

sponsible for the death of Jesus. Indeed, in Araujo's mind, all of us must share the blame. Also, having grown up with the Bible from Genesis through Revelation, he knew prophecy and the Jewish origins of Jesus.

And Araujo knows how to get things done, with diplomacy, tact, and a fiery determination when it is necessary. "He has been a marvelous diplomat in putting this thing together," the theologian Wes Brown has said often about Araujo.

After he received tacit approval from Jerusalem Mayor Teddy Kollek to pursue the project in his beloved city, Araujo sought out Christians and Jewish leaders in the community for advice and counsel. He knew instinctively that the slightest indiscretion with the script or its staging could stop the play before it started.

Dr. M. Bernard Resnikoff was one of the first Jewish leaders from whom Araujo sought counsel. An American from New Jersey, Bernie Resnikoff is head of the Israel office of the American Jewish Committee. From his office on ancient Ethiopia Street, Resnikoff has for fifteen years been working to

Everything, to the last detail of their costumes, had to be correct for each and every performance.

improve relations between Christians and Jews, between Jews and Muslims, and among Jews themselves. He is a practicing Orthodox Jew himself. His sense of history, knowledge of religion, and compassion for people are unusual. There is something about just being in Jerusalem that enhances these characteristics in a man, it seems.

Early one morning in mid-October I met with Resnikoff in his office to share his impressions of Israel, the remarkable city of Jerusalem, the Passion Play, and the future of human relations in the Holy Land. It was the beginning of the Jewish holiday called Succoth, the Feast of Tabernacles. Two weeks later Francisco de Araujo and his gallant band of players would meet at St. Peter en Gallicantu to present their closing-night performance.

Resnikoff explained that the seventy-five-year-old American Jewish Committee had opened its Jerusalem office during the 1960s in the hope that, one way or another, its accumulated wisdom and experience might help Israel to solve its problems.

The "problem" in Israel is special.

"That's because although a Jew from Jersey and a Jew from Iraq living in Jerusalem may be bound together by religion, history, tradition, and life itself, they are terribly divided by culture, styles of living, and value systems."

When this condition is compounded by the presence of so many other peoples of differing colors, reli-

gions, languages, even school systems, it is extremely difficult to find the right way to bridge the gap, to facilitate communication.

"Sometimes we fail. Pretty often we fail," Resnikoff admits. "But there is always enough by-product to stimulate you to go on."

As he spoke, in his strong and precise manner, Resnikoff referred one moment to "these people" (those who had founded the State of Israel) and the next to "us" because he now considers himself a citizen of Israel.

What problems there are within the country, he explained, are mostly a result of the newness of the sovereign experience.

"These people have not had a sovereign state for thousands of years. The people who were living then are not living now. And they didn't write any books about how it is done. They are starting from scratch, in a way. All of our literature is about how to make it in a hostile environment. So we don't know how to do this damn thing. We really don't know yet how to run the country."

One encounters this kind of self-effacing attitude about their achievement as a democratic society among many Israelis. All the more remarkable that theirs is so advanced a democracy compared with other nations of the Middle East.

I asked Resnikoff about that aspect of Israeli society that presented an area of concern to the producers of the Passion Play: the struggle to find ways to accommodate the differences between religious and nonreligious Jews, those who might have objected violently to the play's coming to Jerusalem and those to whom its coming would be welcomed as a fine cultural event, nothing more.

He admitted that a way had not been found yet to reconcile those differences. "That is why you still see evidence of friction and turmoil and turbulence," he said. "It will continue. It is because we're only thirty-three years old and we haven't made it yet.

However, looking from the perspective of history, one might say that the Americans haven't made it yet. It is now her 205th year. How many Americans are still deprived of 'life, liberty and the pursuit of happiness'? Whether it is the Chicanos, the Blacks, or whatever. Don't forget what we did to our own Japanese-Americans in World War II."

Then this philosophical Israeli-American Jew pleaded rhetorically: "Americans ought to be a little bit more understanding of the acknowledged difficulties this country is having. The Jewish people are more than a religion. They are also a civilization."

Seizing on the fact that this day marked the beginning of the Feast of Tabernacles, Succoth, my Jewish friend had found a splendid example of his claim. Of the many Jewish feasts, only three were made obligatory by God as the Jews wandered forty years in the Sinai desert: Passover, Pentecost, and Succoth. Considered by many to be the most important festival, the latter is a time of supreme happiness and rejoicing. Succoth kept alive for the Jews God's promise to bring them into a land "flowing with milk and honey." It was a prophetic feast.

About Succoth the words of John (7:37–38) send a message to Christians: "In the last day, that great day of the feast Jesus stood and cried saying, 'If any man thirst, let him come unto me and drink. He that believeth in me, out of his innermost being shall flow rivers of living water.'"

Resnikoff continued: "The religious Jew shares with the not-so-religious Jew certain traditions and practices even though they are respected for different reasons. For example, here we are in the Feast of Succoth (Tabernacles). This is a religious description. The religious Jews build a tabernacle (or booth of palm and growing things in which the bounty of the land is displayed), because that is what the Lord commanded. But the nonreligious Jews also build tabernacles, not because the Lord commanded but because it is part of their history and part of the culture.

"Back in the United States either you are religious or you are not. Here it is a crazy mixture where certain trappings of religion overlay the secular world." Once again I concluded it is not easy to separate a Jew from his religion or his religion from the Jew.

Turning to the Passion Play itself, Resnikoff praised the Lord that the first season had about passed without incident. "Even though there are no textural or rational reasons to object to the Play, there are emotional factors

They were more than actors. They made costumes, sold tickets, and helped one another to overcome the loneliness and doubt.

that are still to be concerned about." He seemed to be saying that they would be hovering about for some time to come.

Resnikoff said: "There are so many here who still remember how they suffered at the hands of Gentiles . . . they are not ready to face the Christians again. I am not pleased by it, but I understand it when one of these Jews has said to me, 'Hey, Christmas came around this year and I didn't even know.' That's not so much an anti-Christian thing. It's just a reaction to all of the years that he had to 'celebrate' Christmas because he was part of a Christian society. Here the Christians can worship and celebrate as they wish, but it's not an overwhelming, dominating presence. To many Jews this kind of independence is a comforting thing. In a sense, that is why I think that so many Jews are not ready yet for the Passion Play of Jerusalem."

But confront the Christians they must and hope for the best whenever they may be exposed to the brilliant, supersensitive production that Araujo has created. As evidence of Araujo's sensitivity, Resnikoff cited the occasion when the Washington musician closed the Play on the night of a Jewish holiday. "He didn't have to close. It wasn't a Christian holiday and there are no regulations saying that he had to close. He just did it out of respect for his hosts."

About the Play itself, Resnikoff says: "It is great. I was deeply moved by it. I was absolutely enthralled. As a believing, practicing Jew I could find virtually nothing offensive in it. And I am a Jew who used to wince at the sound of the name Jesus."

And then Resnikoff put his finger on the central issue to him: the reason why it has been so helpful to interfaith relations that Francisco de Araujo brought his production to Jerusalem. He said:

"Jerusalem is where Christians, and Jews, should experience the Passion the way Araujo has done it. In this city it is possible because it is his city and it is my city. We were both born here in a spiritual sense. Here we can share Jesus and we can share the land and we can share the Holy Book. . . .

"If you want to understand your Jesus you've got to come to me. If we Jews didn't think about Jesus, you Christians couldn't possibly relate to one of us. Jesus lived like we do, like some of us still live today.

"If you want to understand how he developed, what made him think the way he did and how his disciples thought, we've got the answers. Please come to us."

Resnikoff went on to describe a new kind of dialogue that he sees developing in Jerusalem between Christians and Jews. If it continues and spreads it could bring about a kind of revolution of the human spirit. How prophetic that it is happening in the land of Jesus, after two thousand years of misunderstanding. I have witnessed the examples that Resnikoff used to illustrate this small but significant beginning of reconciliation.

"There are Christians in this city," continued the American Jewish Committee director, "for whom Christianity is no question. They are not toying with something else. They are totally committed Christians who have studied Hebrew, who have begun to speak Hebrew, who can think and dream in Hebrew.

"They are beginning to study the classical Hebrew texts in order to better understand the New Testament environment out of which Christianity came forth and to get at the roots of their Christianity. Without demeaning their Christianity in any way, they are finding a way of reaching back to a time before things got off the track and to discover that all of their books relate to the same thing: God."

To balance the picture of reconciliation as he sees it, Resnikoff then told of a professor at the Hebrew University, in Jerusalem, who is an expert in and teaches about the New Testament.

His voice rising, Resnikoff said: "This man is pious, he is devout, he prays every day in the synagogue, he is very orthodox . . . and he teaches in the Hebrew University, the University of the Jewish people! Here is an Orthodox Jew teaching in the Hebrew language to Jewish kids in the University of the Jewish people . . . teaching them the story of Jesus.

"This man has written books on Jesus as a person that are so profound that Christians from the world over come to sit at his feet and learn about their Lord and Master. He is so immersed in the life of Jesus that this Orthodox Jew has said, 'I love Jesus.' "

Later in that day of Succoth, the Feast of Tabernacles, in his somewhat Spartan but pleasant office at Tantur, I asked Wes Brown about the Judeo-Christian rift and the outlook for reconciliation.

During his more than twenty years

of missionary work in Africa, theological study in California, and living with the Bible and its people in Israel, Brown has become quite sensitized to the reality of the problem, if not overly optimistic about the chances for solution.

Leaning toward me so that his soft voice could be heard, Brown said: "The fault is not Jesus' fault. The fault is of the multitude of people who dare to bear his name as Christians but whose lives and relationships absolutely deny the Lord that they supposedly proclaim. That is the tragedy of it. When people come back to Jesus himself, by and large, we do not have these problems.

"Some of us Christians, like myself, are so overwhelmed by the reading of the history of what many so-called Christians did (to the Jews) that when we confront Jewish people who have been scared by all this we're almost traumatized into silence. Then one realizes that we can't live boxed into the past.

"Being Christian also involves acceptance of God's pardon of whatever the nature of our collective guilt might be. By accepting God's pardon and by beginning to relate to the Jewish people in a sensitive, compassionate way ... by God's grace, maybe we can become agents of healing instead of hurt."

Brown agreed with his Orthodox Jewish friend Resnikoff that the Passion Play of Jerusalem would help those in its audience to see more clearly the person of Jesus and his relationship to the Jews.

The tall, slender Californian spoke with enthusiasm about Araujo's Passion Play and with hope about the impact it might have. He attached special meaning and significance to the message of purpose that the producers of the Passion Play printed with the play's program. It said:

"We believe it is time to bury forever the distorted notion that any one race or group of people should be blamed generally for the crucifixion of Jesus Christ.

"One of the aims of the Passion Play of Jerusalem is to be true to the Bible in showing that no one group of people can be accused of the death of Christ.

"Some of history's most ignominious atrocities have been committed on the gallows of this perverted rationalization.

"If all Jews are guilty of Christ's crucifixion through Caiaphas and his compatriots, then all Gentiles should be blamed through the deeds of Pontius Pilate and his compatriots.

"But Christ Himself prayed, while on the cross, for all humanity: 'Father, forgive them, for they know not what they do. . . .' The people at the foot of the cross, who heard that prayer, and for whom it was spoken, were of a variety of races and groups.

"Clearly, it is contrary to the spirit of Christ, whom Christians worship, to blame Jews or Gentiles *en masse* for Christ's death.

"Christians believe that, as the Apostle Paul wrote, ' . . . the wages of sin is death.' Christianity teaches that Christ died to collect that wage for all human beings who would accept the atonement.

"Proper Christian doctrine, then, holds that if there is responsibility to be charged for the death of Christ, it should be laid on all humanity, for, writes the Apostle, all have sinned and come short of the glory of God."

Wes Brown called the statement "immensely sensitive and important," as indeed it was. Because relatively few Jews in Jerusalem would actually see the Play during the first season, the statement was crucial in assuaging the fears of many in high places that the Play would be just like all the rest.

The statement was written by the Reverend Wallace Henley, pastor of the McElwain Baptist Church, in Birmingham, Alabama, and leader of the congregation that included Frank Parsons, the play's sponsor. From the moment of his decision to sponsor the play, Parsons had sought the help of his pastor to navigate the shoals of difficulty he knew to be ahead. Obviously a committed Christian, Wally Henley had also been a newspaperman and had served on the White House staff during the administration of President Richard Nixon. Henley knew well the murky history of Judeo-Christian relations, even though he had never been to the land of Israel. He also knew well the value of good public relations—in business, government, or religion.

Founded in faith, crafted with conviction, and epitomized by the Play itself, the statement was received in Israel invariably with great appreciation by both Christians and Jews. It said to them that Araujo and his courageous little company were in Jerusalem, where it all began, to turn over a new page and not to repeat those things that have hurt Jewish people in the past.

Teddy Kollek, the legendary mayor of Jerusalem, was one of those to whom the message and the spirit embodied by Francisco de Araujo and his Passion Play were critically important.

Kollek has been mayor of Jerusalem since 1965, two years before the Six-Day War, which established many of the borders, administrative boundaries, and occupied zones of Israel that bedevil politicians to this day. Jerusalem's administrative parameters were among those established then. In one fell swoop the forces of Jordan were driven from the West Bank of the Jordan River and East Jerusalem and the city was reunited under Israeli sovereignty . . . and the guidance of Teddy Kollek.

From that time forward Kollek has applied four principles to his administration of Jerusalem. As he recounts them:

1. There shall be free access to all the holy places irrespective of nationality and they shall be administered by their adherents.

2. Everything possible shall be done to ensure unhindered develop-

ment of the Arab way of life in the Arab sections of the city and ensure Muslims and Christians a practical religious, cultural, and commercial governance over their own lives.

3. Everything possible should be done to ensure equal governmental, municipal, and social services in all parts of the city.

4. Continuing efforts should be made to increase cultural, social, and economic contacts among the various elements of Jerusalem's population, while preserving the cultural and even the national identity of each group.

Through unswerving devotion to these principles and the kind of energy that exhausts those around him, Kollek has made the Holy City, the city of David, a city of the moment while enhancing its ancient biblical character. Kollek has helped the government of Israel and those who govern that democratic society to realize their dreams of greatness for their beloved capital. And be assured, Jerusalem is the capital of Israel. It will remain so until the end of time. On that point there is no disagreement among the people of Israel, regardless of their differences on other matters of internal or external affairs.

For those to whom Israel is home, either from birth or as émigrés, the city is a good place to live, to work, to rest, and to worship. Teddy Kollek and successive state governments have seen to that.

When the Israeli Government confirmed the fact that Jerusalem is the capital of Israel, by its passage of the so-called Jerusalem Law, in 1980, the international reaction was negative. Thirteen nations moved their embassies to Tel Aviv in protest against the law. They saw it as premature and in contrast to previous agreement to negotiate the future status of the city and its West Bank Arab population.

Writing about those events in the American journal *Foreign Affairs,* Teddy Kollek remembers: "I had personally objected to the Jerusalem Law as unnecessary and needlessly provocative; but once its passage seemed assured, I appeared before the Knesset Law Committee and at my request a paragraph was added as follows: 'The Holy Places shall be protected against any desecration or any other sacrilege or anything which is apt to interfere with the freedom of access of all religious adherents to their Holy Places or to injure their feelings towards these places.'"

Perhaps because of this effort and others with community leaders after the Law's passage, everyday life in the city was not affected.

While determined to help maintain a united Jerusalem as capital of Israel, Kollek insists that the city and State governments will continue to give Arabs and the various other religious communities there wide freedom of speech, religion, education, and access and movement.

Says Kollek: "These freedoms are based on the self-denial of our own sovereign rights in these fields. These unilateral acts have been taken because we believe in principle in these democratic and religious freedoms for everyone."

Teddy Kollek has his detractors. All politicians have them. But Teddy Kollek is respected more widely than are most politicians. He is impressive for his physical energy, his ability to anticipate problems and deal with them decisively, and his understanding of the Jewish composition of his city.

It is not unusual for him to request meetings with petitioners at six in the morning or for him to return important calls in the middle of the night. He has little time for small talk and can be pretty gruff at times. But, those who know him well insist, the Jerusalem mayor can also be sensitive to the smallest personal details of life. A friend remembers the evening that Kollek would not talk business until he had climbed on a chair to set free a small songbird that had been trapped behind a window blind.

After the Six-Day War, while others in the city were still reeling from the heady wine of victory, Teddy went tearing into the Old City to call on every church, Christian and non-Christian. He went to reassure them, to determine the extent of damage, and to offer help in restoration. He wanted all to know that the spirit of tranquillity, so important to Jerusalem, would be restored quickly.

"Though Teddy is not a religious Jew, he is a great man," says Bernie Resnikoff. "He knows that this city summons up emotions more than any other for Christians, Muslims, and Jews. Most important, he understands the way different kinds of Jews respond to this city and its magic."

The result, Resnikoff suggests, is that Teddy Kollek has the trust of all segments of Jerusalem society: religious Jews, Christians, Muslims, and the secularists. Nearly fifteen years of relative calm and prosperity in the city indicate that their trust has been well placed.

Kollek himself was somewhat less sanguine about matters when he wrote in *Foreign Affairs*:

"The mood of the city has changed in these last few years, sometimes for the better but not always so. For one thing, there has been an increased religious awareness among Jews, Christians and Muslims; but Jews and Arabs, while living next to each other, have not grown much closer. Many Jewish families who came from Arab countries often have unhappy memories of the regimes whose oppressive and discriminatory measures they escaped and whom they sometimes cannot help but identify with Arabs here. On the other hand, no matter how much Jerusalem's Arabs may, in their heart of hearts, appreciate the economic upswing, the tranquillity, the improved educational and municipal facilities, the massive tourism of the united city, few Arabs can be expected to be enthusiastic about the perpetuation of their status as a minority and the absence of a long-term political solution for the area or the city. And the current inflation has also somewhat reduced the economic gains from which they have benefited."

Is there an answer to the question of Jerusalem? Can a solution be found to the problem of the West Bank and East Jerusalem, where the Arabs live and where most of the city's holy places are? No one seems to know. Perhaps the most philosophical answer, which I've heard from many, was best given by Bernie Resnikoff:

"There are some problems in life that have no solution. Not everything in life has to have a solution, and it is just possible that this is one of them. If I am right, then all we can hope for here is to coexist in a condition of permanent armed truce.

"I never expect this city to become a homogeneous population, with shared, common interests. It will likely always be divided in terms of lifestyles, clothing, work habits, food preferences, political allegiances, and spiritual dimensions.

"But if I can continue to feel perfectly comfortable going into the Old City at eleven o'clock at night without looking over my shoulder, maybe that is enough. If my son can be out at midnight without my worrying and the Arab parents can feel the same way, then maybe we have something."

The very real and perpetual tensions facing Israel and its capital seemed very far away that day of the last night with Jesus and the Passion Play. As the daylight hours passed there in the courtyard of St. Peter en Gallicantu, so, too, had the threat of rain passed.

A brilliant blue sky over the Holy City now set a canvas to display cumulus clouds moving swiftly from west to east. Their shadows formed puddles of dark gray on the hills and valleys as they flew over us. One moment the Kidron Valley was dark. The next it came alive with sunlight. Beyond the valley the Mount of Olives, where Jesus had walked and spoken to his disciples, shimmered in light as of an Impressionist painting. Then it, too, turned gray.

The only sounds came from a barking dog belonging to one of the Arab homeowners on the hill and from Max Jacoby as he asked in pleasantly accented English for an actor to move this way or that in order that he might get a better photograph.

It was growing cooler in the long shadow that covered the courtyard as the sun raced to set. Soon night would come, with the abruptness of a window shade being pulled down. Then it would be cold enough for a sweater and jacket. Maybe a blanket for the legs as well.

Oh, Jesus, I thought, how cold you must have been in the dungeon on that hill the night before your supreme sacrifice. And how cold it would be for the young actors as they re-created his story that night. But they had suffered together before, and suffered well, since their first meetings with Francisco de Araujo, many months before.

The core group of eight had been recruited by Araujo in the United States. They came from such places as Seattle, Los Angeles, Birmingham, Alabama, and Washington, D.C. In Israel they were joined by kids from Jerusalem, Tantur, and Bethlehem. They were American, Arab, and Jew. In several tongues they tried to speak a language of love, for each other and for the story they were telling.

Their leader and the first to join Araujo's quest was a remarkable young man from Everett, Washington, Gregory Allen Strom. Little did he know when he first met the impassioned Araujo that he, Greg Strom, would become Jesus of Nazareth. The experience would change his life.

Until his senior year at Whitworth College, Greg thought he might become a professional football player, a defensive backfield position called strong safety. At that position in American football, the first thing one learns is the need to hit the opposing player as hard as one can hit, to dislodge the football from his outstretched hands or to punish him if he catches the ball before you can stop him. It is hard, physically demanding work. There is little time to think about anything but brute force and preventing one's opponent from reaching his goal. Greg Strom was good enough at what he did in football to have received a college scholarship. And he was recruited by two of the well-known professional teams: the Dallas Cowboys and the hometown Seattle Seahawks.

Then the Good Lord intervened, according to Greg. He was injured in an off-the-field accident that stunned his lower back. "It was the Lord's providence," remembers Strom. "It was very hard for me to take. It closed off my professional football opportunities."

The event opened another course, which he would follow soon after. While still in his senior year at Whitworth, Greg capitalized on his studies in radio and television and took a part-time job with the CBS affiliate in Spokane, Washington, to learn the broadcast business first-hand. The year was 1979.

In October of that year he applied for and got a job during the Christmas recess managing an exhibition booth at the 1980 meeting of the National Religious Broadcasters in Washington, D.C. The assignment would be his first trip east of the state of Idaho. And it would lead to his first contact with Francisco de Araujo.

The ruggedly handsome young man remembers that first meeting with Araujo with amusement. One of the conductor's early sponsors had taken a small booth to announce the Passion Play and to entice investors from the attending travel agents.

Anxious to ensure that things were done right with his booth, Araujo arrived at the convention site early to check it out. To his dismay he found that his booth had not yet been set up. Furious, he demanded to see the manager regarding the oversight.

Hearing the Araujo outburst, one of his assistants came to Greg Strom and said, "There is a man out there who is demanding to see the manager. You'd better do something."

Strom went to Araujo and asked if he could help.

Araujo said: "I don't want to talk to you. I want to talk to the manager."

"I'm sorry, sir, but I am the manager," Greg said in his soft voice and quiet manner.

Strom admits that he spent more time listening than talking during the first conversation with Araujo. But, in the end, he did succeed in calming the perturbed director and left him there with his assistant, thinking it was the last he would see of the white-haired man.

"Two days later," Strom recalls with a laugh, "another assistant came to me with a note from a man called Francisco, or was it a man from San Francisco? Imagine my surprise when the man turned out to be Araujo."

Filled with apologies for the earlier run-in, Araujo asked Strom if he had yet seen the sights of Washington and, if not, would he like to join Araujo on a tour.

The two spent the rest of that day going from one monument to the next. Araujo combined commentary about American history with a kind of interview of Strom.

"We went finally to the Smithsonian, had a soft drink, and talked a bit more about what I wanted to do with my career. We exchanged addresses and said so long. We hit it off very quickly and very tightly."

The meeting started a relationship that would be carried on through letters and telephone conversations during the next few months, the last in Strom's senior year of college. During that time Araujo would get no closer to realizing his dream of producing the Jerusalem Passion Play.

After graduation, Greg "did a few things in television for my college" while he looked for a permanent job with one of the commercial television operations on the West Coast. He had put any thought of working with

Araujo out of his mind. But Araujo remembered.

In October he called Strom and asked him to fly to Washington, at his own expense, to assist in the production of the Nativity Play that Christmas on the Ellipse, behind the White House and adjacent to the National Christmas Tree. It is a production for which Araujo has been well known and applauded for many years.

Knowing that the younger man had only enough money to cover the air fare, Araujo invited Strom to stay at his house in Lanham, Maryland—for the duration of their work together.

Greg soon enough discovered that working with Araujo on a production is more than learning theater. He spent the better part of his time raising the money required to stage the Nativity Play.

Faced with a go–no-go decision about the play on December 1, the two had fallen short of their financial goal.

"We decided to go ahead anyway, on faith," Strom recalls.

With his many other chores during the play, Strom became an actor, of sorts. Because he was an experienced horseman, Strom played a Roman soldier in the Nativity story. He also became Araujo's aide and confidant as the director continued to pursue his dream of the Jerusalem Passion Play. The make-or-break 1981 convention of religious broadcasters was only a month away.

At midnight, after each performance of the Nativity, behind the White House, the two friends went home to Lanham and worked until four in the morning on the Passion Play. Their effort at this point focused on the sound track of the play. It would form the basis of the play itself, which Araujo would later bring to life through staging and direction on location in Jerusalem.

Strom, because of his experience with audio recording, sound mixing, and other technical aspects of broad-casting, was given the assignment to bring all the pieces together in the studio. With Araujo at his side, he spent in excess of one hundred studio hours at the task.

The sound track would eventually combine more than one hundred pieces of music, narration, and a score of voices, which the actors in Jerusalem would later be required to mime.

It was arduous, frustrating work, work that might have caused a novice of lesser motivation to abandon the effort at any time. Months later, in Jerusalem, I asked Greg what was going through his mind during the winter of 1981, when the reality of the Passion Play was still so distant and the financing still not in hand.

He answered: "There has always been a sense in me that as long as I am sensitive to what the Lord wants me to do—which I've not always been—then he would carve out a niche for me that was right, even though it might be different from that which I expected for myself. This was certainly different. But it was right."

And it remained right, even during the hours and days and months of struggle, sacrifice, and self-doubt that lay ahead, according to the ex-football player now turned actor and show-man.

There were times, Strom confesses, when it would have been easier to say, "Forget it, this thing is taking my soul and I don't know if I am going to regain it."

Such thoughts were far from his mind, however, when Araujo first asked him to play the role of Jesus Christ. The question came at two in the morning, during a break in one of their all-night sessions and just as Greg was about to apply syrup to his break-fast pancakes.

"I was so shocked, I just looked up at Francisco in amazement, and poured the syrup all over the plate, the table, and me," he says. At that moment Greg realized that he had become involved not only with something different but something that would test his creative spirit, his physical stamina, his human resolve—and his faith.

"This," says Greg, "was not just another play, nor was it just another passion play." It was a play in which Greg's own image of Jesus would be matched by that of Francisco de Araujo. Not surprisingly, that image is one of a man who was "extremely capable physically."

Says Greg: "He must have been capable physically in order to take the punishment that he took and still be able to do what he had to do during the last hours of his Passion. Many people, I believe, would have physically died from the beating he suffered *before* the crucifixion. What we wanted to show was this physical strength, as well as his spiritual strength. Through this portrayal of Jesus, though beaten and broken, with dirt in his beard and briars in his hair, we wanted people to see his eyes—the inner strength that made him more than an ordinary man."

Strom's image of Jesus is more than that, of course. It would have to be, considering the fact that the young American lived the last days of Jesus every day and almost every night for six months on Mount Zion itself.

Jesus is to Strom very kind, very loving, extremely understanding, but not a great scholar. "He knew the Old Testament like the back of his hand, and the Talmud. But he was not an intellectual," according to the actor-student.

Most important to this young Christian who has never heard of Ernie Levy, Jesus the Nazarene was an "extremely just man."

Says Strom: "I think he was just to the point that we are often confused by it. Many times when he would rebuke somebody, people through the ages have not really known for sure why he did. All we know is that, in spite of his rebukes and sometimes hard positions on one aspect or another of our behavior, he continues to deal with us in a just manner—if we let him."

The Lord was constant and consistent in his beliefs and teachings to a point that none of us can comprehend, let alone emulate, observes Strom. "Just acting the role of Jesus for several hours a day was almost too much to give," he says. "Imagine being that way every day of your life, for a lifetime."

As with many persons who have, from time to time through history, found themselves doing something in his name and for his glory, Greg Strom had no special training for the task. It

is simply that he is a Christian. For as long as he can recall, "Jesus has been number one" in his life.

He remembers that when he was a junior in high school one of his counselors called him a "religious vagabond." He was confirmed in the Lutheran Church. But he also attended a Baptist church, went to a Pentecostal church for a while, and attended a Presbyterian school. He also was a member of a charismatic movement. He describes his religious background as "interdenominational and nondenominational."

Through it all, he says, "I have had an intense respect and desire for Jesus Christ. I remember making decisions toward Christianity when I was only

Even the young man who would play the role of Jesus lent a hand to set up scenery for the Nativity Play in Bethlehem.

nine years old. There has never been any other thought with me."

As a Protestant Christian he was familiar mostly with the New Covenant. Not until he arrived in the Holy Land did he begin to study the Old Testament with intensity. He was, after all, about to portray the life of a Jewish prophet. The more he immersed himself in the role and in the Scriptures, the more clearly he remembered a time when he had moved away from Jesus. It was during the last two years of college. For a time, he could not reconcile the worldly thoughts of the great philosophers with the ancient Gospels.

Says Greg: "What brought me back to Jesus is that I had gone so far away from him that all of what he was and represented came right around and hit me in the back. It happened because I finally realized that he could not have lied about what he was and what there was waiting for those of us who believed. He just did not have the capacity to lie."

It is, one supposes, as with the confessions made by any dying man—about his guilt or innocence, his love or longing for that which was or might have been. The things that Jesus said as he went to his death could not have been lies. There had to be truth in those words and thoughts recorded by several then and debated by so many more ever since.

It is said that many actors become the persons they are portraying. Their involvement with the character is so intense. It makes the difference between just acting and a great performance. I know of no one who has not thought Greg Strom's portrayal of Jesus is a great performance. It follows that he must have become "Christlike" in the process.

"If I had not tried to become Christlike I would never have been able to deliver a convincing performance. And I would have become schizophrenic," Strom says.

For a young, "macho" American who has made it on the playing fields of many football stadiums and in personal struggles with a confusing and confused twentieth-century society, it was not always easy to be "Christlike."

In difficult encounters with others in the cast, to whom he is a kind of boss as well as the lead player, and with those from the community who did not want the Play going on at all, Strom was tested several times. From the latter there were even threats to his and Araujo's lives. The issue of the Passion Play was, at times, *that* emotional.

On those occasions "the old man" in Greg, the man that would have previously struck back, violently, at the challenge, lost out to the "new man" in him. He did, he insists, respond with patience, even love. And it worked, he says.

The closeness of Gregory Allen Strom to Jesus of Nazareth perhaps reached its zenith the night before opening night in the premier season of the Jerusalem Passion Play. That night, sponsor Frank Parsons, Rev. Wally Henley, and Francisco de Araujo gave a dinner for Greg and the other American members of the cast. It was an emotional affair. Parsons spoke of his gratitude to all of them and for the opportunity to have made their labor possible. Araujo exhorted all to do their best in the spirit of the Passion. Henley led the group in prayer. One could feel the warmth of Jesus' presence. All retired for a night of well-deserved rest.

All, that is, except Greg Strom.

At about two in the morning, Greg Strom left the Hilton with his Bible and drove to the Church of St. Peter en Gallicantu—to pass the night, alone, in the dungeon where Jesus had been held the night before the Crucifixion.

As Greg relates the story of that night: "I went to the church, parked the car, and locked it. With the gold key to the church I opened the great wood-and-metal door and entered. I left the lights off, because I thought to light them would somehow defile the experience.

"To reach the dungeon from the main floor of the church you have to take several sets of stairs, to the right and then to the left and to the right again. The sleeping bag I had brought with me began to unravel as I trod downward. I thought, 'It's like a horror movie or something.' "

This young traveler into the past made a few wrong turns, one of which took him into the courtyard "where Peter denied Christ."

"I went then back up the stairs," Greg recalls, "and finally felt my way into the dungeon. When I found that room I knew it was the place, even though I couldn't see a thing.

"I went to the floor and laid out the sleeping bag and my little alarm clock—that I had brought to be sure that I wasn't there sleeping when the tourists came, in the morning.

"I started to have a quiet little worship.

"Then I got up and felt my way along the wall of the dungeon to the place where the figure of the Crucifixion has emerged. I spent some time pressed up against it."

Time passed quickly for the young pilgrim in the dungeon where Jesus had slept. When he did try to sleep it was already four in the morning. The sun would be up soon.

But he did not sleep, as he thought he would. Instead, he remembers:

"My body began pulsating, slowly, with sensations of warmth and comfort. It was cold. But I was warm.

"At about five in the morning, from inside the church, I heard the most wonderful, supernatural songs from somewhere. There were echoing voices of song.

"I lay there, suspended, until seven-thirty, when the alarm went off. I realized then that I had not slept all night.

Still, when I left the dungeon that morning I was rested. I came out of the dungeon without sleeping a wink all night, and yet I was completely refreshed from the last four months of work. I was ready for the opening night. It had been 107 days since we had had one day off.

"The night before, when Wally Henley led us in silent prayer, I prayed, 'Lord, please give rest to my weary, tired bones, because it has really been hard.' I was granted that."

Greg was not granted the kind of anonymity off the stage that his shy nature might have preferred. In fact, in the Old City of Jerusalem and in many places of the new city he has been recognized with his beard and long hair of the first century and called out to often. From the shops and in eating places they have called out to him, "Hello, Jesus."

"At first," he says, "it was so uncomfortable for me. I felt so unworthy. Later I learned to take it as an act of kindness."

In a lighter moment I asked the young actor/producer if he didn't get a kick out of the recognition.

"No, I really don't," he answered. "I don't get a kick out of being known here as Jesus. It is too much responsibility. I am Greg, not Jesus."

The play in which Greg Strom starred and to which he and his American and Holy Land compatriots devoted so much time and effort is perhaps the most innovative theater ever attempted.

It combines grand, sweeping exposure to the classics of classical music with ample bites of the most inspirational passages from contemporary movie scores. There is even an exquisitely performed rendition of the Negro spiritual "Were You There," to enhance those moments of reflection after the crucifixion scenes.

Events from the story of Jesus and his Passion are staged with an attention to detail that make them reach out to the audience, making it a part of the happening. Words and music do not provide simply a backdrop for each scene. They stun the mind, causing it to soar with emotion and curiosity.

Many scenes, the Last Supper for example, are executed so as to bring to life great works of art, great paintings and sculpture. In the last moments of these scenes the actors freeze in positions which, if photographed, would seem to be the Last Supper of Da Vinci or the Pietà by Michelangelo.

The lighting, engineered by the Israeli television producer Uzi Pelled and directed by Araujo, is inspired. Pelled also assembled the complicated sound system. Araujo employs his lighting as a muralist, throwing a pin spot into one corner of a scene while he washes with a softer light a look at a scene to come.

Unless one is reminded, it is hard to accept that the actors are not actually speaking their sacred words, barking commands, or hurling epithets at one another. They are in fact miming the script. Here, again, Araujo has worked miracles with his players. It is one thing to lip-synch a song. It is done often on television. It is quite another thing to combine this lip-voice synchronization with the most precise and convincing facial expressions and body movements; actions that communicate inner pain, suffering, despair, or wonderment. All of this, Araujo's actors do with a vengeance.

Araujo is not content to employ only these facets of the performing arts, which would be pageant enough for most directors. He has also used the art of ballet to send his message. And that message had to somehow deal with the question of blame for the crucifixion. The device concocted by Araujo to deal with this challenge is a stroke of genius to all who see it.

They are called the tormentors by some. They are demons to others. *They* are a company of dancers who portray the embodiment of evil in all of us. The evil that caused Jew to turn against Jew two thousand years ago; evil that caused Him to be misunderstood and crucified. Evil that has caused many Christians since then to misinterpret, even deny his word.

Dressed in rags, made up with hideous masks, the demon dancers leap and grovel, writhe and rant their way through every scene in which there is need to be reminded that we were all responsible for the crucifixion. They are there when he is arrested. They perform their macabre dance during and after his trial. It is they who whip the crowd into a frenzy that leads to his sentence upon the Cross.

Finally, as Jesus dies on the Cross, the dancers fall to the ground, twisted and spent. For as he died, so did the evil of that terrible moment die. The scene leaves the viewer unable to move or to breathe. The message is overpowering. We have seen what Jesus meant when he said from the Cross, "It is finished."

But the Play does not end there. The resurrection is still to come. And it comes with all the power and joy that Araujo can muster from his players and his musical inspiration. Great light flashes from his tomb. The earth shakes, or so it seems. His followers run to spread the Good News. All of this against the towering and familiar Hallelujah Chorus, by Handel. The moment is enough to cause even the most jaded Christian in the audience to come to his or her feet.

Curiously, when the performance comes to a close there is no applause. Only stunned silence, for the longest moments. There are tears. But there is no other sound. The audience is spent, emotionally and spiritually. They know that they have just seen a great spectacle, a superb evening of theater, shared the music of many masters. Bravos and loud applause are not appropriate to the end of this play.

When and where did these many ideas and creative flashes originate in the ever-active mind of Francisco de Araujo, these ideas that move audience and critic alike to sit in stunned silence when the experience is behind them?

He says that scenes just "pop" into his head while he was conducting great religious music live in concert halls. During the furious chorus "He trusted in God" from Handel's *Messiah* the demons appeared on the stage of his mind. To him, the crucifixion comes to life as he listens to the inspired opening of the Verdi *Requiem*.

"I knew when I first led my choral society in 'Were You There' that I would use that music in something," Araujo says. "Then, as I listened to it again during the assembly of our scripts and sound track, the idea to use it with the re-creation of the Michelangelo Pietà came to mind. It happens this way because I am always searching for the meaning of the music, what the music is trying to say."

Araujo is at a loss to explain how the music of the Passion Play came together so beautifully. He wondered—agonized might be a better word—often how he would be able to "throw all those forces together."

Not surprisingly, the actual staging of each scene could not be done until the director and his little troupe arrived on location in Jerusalem to begin rehearsals. Then it was a race against the clock to be ready for opening night, on August first. The fine tuning of the drama then took place in what Araujo calls "the white heat of inspiration of the moment."

One of the most unusual and effective dramatic devices to be forged in that white heat was the decision not to show Jesus on the Cross at any time during the Play. Instead, after he is seen being nailed to the ghastly device, as he is being lifted up between Heaven and Earth, the stage is suddenly enveloped in darkness. Three crosses on a distant hill are backlit in a dramatic silhouette. When the lights come on again, those at the foot of the Cross, including the dancing demons, are now playing to the audience. The audience becomes part of the mob at the foot of the Cross! The Cross, unseen, is clearly designated somewhere behind them. When Jesus speaks to them at his feet and to his Father the voice comes from behind the audience. The effect is staggering.

In his script, which includes narration and dialogue, Araujo selected what he thought were the most clearly understood and dramatically appealing passages from scripture. The reports of Matthew were used more frequently than those of Mark, Luke, or John. Whenever the actual words of the Bible didn't work dramatically, Araujo wrote his own material, based on the Bible.

Remembering his inner conviction and his pledge to "help heal the wounds of centuries," he chose his Gospel carefully. This was not easy, he says, because so much of the Gospels can be read as anti-Semitic.

"I understand why that is, though," Araujo adds; "the writers were trying to defend their reason for leaving Judaism to start something new."

Commenting from his well-informed vantage point, Wes Brown wrote about the words and music in the Jerusalem *Post,* "A blind person could attend the performance and find the narration, spoken parts and the music of such high quality as to provide a memorable evening."

A memorable evening. With Araujo and Greg Strom, the other young Americans shared more than one hundred memorable evenings after opening night. Who were these young people? What were their impressions of it all as they prepared for closing night in the premier season? In a few days they would leave Jerusalem; to return, God only knew.

Their names read like an honor roll of middle American background and values: John Conway, from Adelphi, Maryland; Barbie Hubbell, of South Gate, California; Kevin Patterson, from Limerick, Maine; Marilou Petrone, from Los Angeles, California; Leslie

Tucker, of Birmingham, Alabama; John Welsh, from Franklin, Pennsylvania; Ajodah (Steve) Seenarine, Jr., of Magnolia, New Jersey.

Protestant Christians all, they knew their Bible about as well as most. Not one had ever been to the Holy Land. They knew little other than what a few college courses had taught them about show business, about the incredible demands that professional theater can make on body and soul. They, too, had become engaged in what their mentor, Francisco de Araujo, referred to so often as pioneer work.

Each thought when recruited by Araujo or Frank Parsons that he or she would be making the journey to Jerusalem to act in the Passion Play. They would soon discover that they would be called upon to do much more. As the permanent staff, they would do everything from helping to build and tear down the bleachers in the amphitheater to selling tickets, changing scenery, and sweeping out the costume room. They would work every day from early morning well into the night, seven days a week, for six months.

There would be little time for a personal life. And the tensions in the ever-threatened land of Israel would be with them every day—quite a change from the comparatively idyllic lives they had left behind in the United States.

They would be thrust, almost daily, into the demanding world of human relations in the Holy Land. Every ounce of patience, diplomacy, and Christian resolve would be called upon and tested. The strain, the culture shock, would leave some of them disillusioned and frustrated about the paradoxes of the land where Jesus lived and spoke the words of peace that they had been raised with.

The opportunity to work with Araujo was considered very special by them all. But they found the director a demanding taskmaster. They had not known before, the fury of a dedicated professional showman. Often they were confused by his internal rage during the white heat of a creative moment. To them all, Araujo is, however, a great artist, perhaps even a genius. Theirs was the typical love-hate relationship of player with director.

They were mystified also by the motives of sponsor Frank Parsons, not able to appreciate fully the struggle he was up against in the financial arena. The mystery affected some more seriously than others. It was their first exposure to the often unpleasant aspects of show *business.*

Through it all, they insist, their spiritual lives have been enriched. Alone and in groups of two or three they had searched the Bible, Old Testament and New, for guidance to better understand themselves and the challenges they faced. One of them, searching in anguish for a way to express what he felt, recalled the words of Paul to the Ephesians (4:29–30): "Guard against foul talk; let your words be for the improvement of others, as occasion offers, and do good to your listeners, otherwise you will only be grieving the Holy Spirit of God. ..."

Perhaps their feelings were summed up best by Steve when he said: "I loved it. I loved the experience. I loved the highs, I loved the lows. Probably, when I look back on it, if I ever get a chance to, I'll see that it was a turning point in my life."

When darkness came to Jerusalem that last night, the sky filled with stars. I wondered why the sky over this holy place always seems to be so brilliant. It can be explained only in part by the clarity of the air.

I was grateful for my old gray sweater and blue windbreaker. It was cold. Then I thought of Greg Strom. He would be very cold tonight, covered only by a loincloth as he portrayed once more the dying Jesus.

Brother Francis was there at the top of the steps leading down to the church and lower still to the amphitheater in the courtyard. He had col-

"React, react! Remember you have just learned that Jesus has been condemned to die on the Cross."

lected tickets at every performance, extending a friendly greeting from behind his neatly goateed face. He had served the Assumptionist Order at the church from the day it was consecrated, in 1931, to commemorate Peter's triple denial of Jesus and his repentance after hearing the cock crow, hence "in Gallicantu."

The gentle and alert priest had been a great help to Araujo and his young American troupers for many months. His knowledge of biblical history seemed boundless, and his sense of the events that took place on the site two thousand years ago was profound.

From the courtyard, one could see now the lights along the top of the wall of the Old City as it climbed sharply from the eastern slope of Mount Zion. Inside the wall was the Jewish Quarter. Treasured by the people of David as evidence of their ancestors' earliest settlement in Jerusalem, the quarter had been burned, ravaged, and razed for centuries by Romans, Muslims, and Christians. In 1948 the quarter was besieged by Arab legionnaires and the Jews driven out. For twenty years the Jews were prohibited by the Jordanians from worshiping at the nearby Western Wall, a violation of the armistice that ended the conflict.

The soft light shining from the area came from the "new" Jewish Quarter, returned to Israel after the Six-Day War, in 1967. The homes being built there now are impressive. Exterior architecture adheres strictly to ancient lines and materials—the lovely sand-white Jerusalem stone. But interior design is the most modern.

Across the Kidron Valley, on the slopes of the Mount of Olives, the lights of countless Arab houses signaled the presence of twentieth-century life there. Somewhere in that valley lay the Garden of Gethsemane, now cloaked in darkness, as well it should be. For it was there that Jesus was arrested after his betrayal by Judas.

Visible, too, were the lights of the Jerusalem Panorama Hotel, where the Passion Play cast had celebrated after opening night, in August. They would have their farewell party there too. From the top-floor restaurant of the hotel they could look back at the lights of Mount Zion and the site where they had labored. Joseph Aweidah, the hotel owner, is a generous man whose family has given lodging to Christian pilgrims since the turn of the century.

A great stillness was upon the land as that night began. Only the sound of an old bus chugging up the Zion mount broke the spell. Soon the night would come alive with the more pleasant and poignant sounds of Bach, Verdi, and Handel. And the stirring words of the Gospels. A friend later told me that these grand sounds could be heard by those who live in the Jewish Quarter. And they were welcome.

Before long the performance would begin and his glory would be portrayed again where it had originally happened, among the Jews, whom he loved.

The dressing room was a scene of controlled chaos. Araujo directed last-minute touches of makeup to disciples and soldiers, harlots and heroines. The tormentors milled about, talking more like the kids they were than the personification of evil they would portray. In a corner sat Hilda Handelman, a good Jewish lady from Pittsburgh, Pennsylvania. She had volunteered to work in the Play after hearing Araujo announce its coming to Jerusalem during an appearance at her temple. She spoke of how much she had enjoyed the experience and her sorrow at its closing. A Messianic Jew, she had come to Israel with her family seven years before. She, too, expressed the hope that the Play would help to bring Christians and Jews closer together.

Amid the din and commotion, Araujo called out to them, "Don't anybody go anywhere yet. I want to have a cast meeting outside. Everyone must attend." Perhaps for the first time since it began, they heeded his command and moved to the parking area, where the tour buses and taxis had just disgorged their passengers, the audience.

Acting now more like an American football coach before a big game than a gifted conductor-director, Araujo rallied his troupe. He thanked them all for a great first season, for their dedication, hard work, and devotion. He introduced Frank Parsons to them as the man who made it all possible. And they cheered. He told them about this book and introduced Max, Hilla, and me. They cheered again.

They were ready to meet the audience, which had now filled the amphitheater. Somewhere Greg Strom was alone, praying to the Lord for the strength he sought.

Moments later, the word of the Lord was heard again in the Holy City, calling out for understanding among men.

Comfort ye, comfort ye my people, saith your God. Speak ye comfortably to Jerusalem, and cry unto her, that her warfare is accomplished, that her iniquity is pardoned....
The voice of him that crieth in the wilderness, Prepare ye the way of the Lord, make straight in the desert a highway for our God.
Every valley shall be exalted. And every hill shall be made low; and the crooked shall be made straight, and the rough places plain.
And the glory of the Lord shall be revealed. And all flesh shall see it together; for the mouth of the Lord hath spoken it.
And there shall come forth a rod out of the stem of Jesse, and a Branch shall grow out of his roots. And the spirit of the Lord shall rest upon him.
The spirit of the Lord is upon me, because He hath anointed me to preach the gospel to the poor; He hath sent me to heal the broken-hearted, to preach deliverance to the captives, and recovering the sight to the blind, to set at liberty them that are bruised. To preach the acceptable year of the Lord.
Who hath believed our report? And to whom is the arm of the Lord revealed?
For he shall grow up before him as a tender plant, and as a root out of the dry ground; and when we shall see him, there is no beauty that we should desire him.
He is despised and rejected of men;

*a man of sorrows; yet we did esteem
him stricken, smitten of God, and
afflicted.
But he was wounded for our
transgressions, he was bruised for
our iniquities: the chastisement of
our peace was upon him; and with
his stripes we are healed.
Thy rebuke hath broken his heart
and he is full of heaviness. He
looked for some to have pity on
him, but there was no man, neither
found he any to comfort him.
Behold and see, behold and see if
there be any sorrow like unto his
sorrow.
He was cut off out of the land of the
living; for the transgressions of
my people was he stricken. And the
Lord hath laid on him the iniquity
of us all.
Behold the Lamb of God, which
taketh away the sin of the world.*

The last performance in the premier
season of the Jerusalem Passion Play
had begun.

January 1, 1982

Postscript

When I was first told about the Jerusalem Passion Play, I could not believe
my ears. Stage a Passion Play on the
very site where the Judeo-Christian
problem started? I thought it was a
joke.

Then I learned that it would be presented with anti-Semitism expunged. I
read the script and heard the music. I
experienced, firsthand, the fierce sin-
cerity of Francisco de Araujo. I studied
the statement of noble intent prepared
by the sponsors. If anything on the
subject of the crucifixion had a chance
to succeed, I concluded, it was the
Jerusalem Passion Play.

Jerusalem's mayor, Teddy Kollek,
had had similar reactions to these factors. And he reached a similar conclusion. His conclusion was not reached
as easily as mine had been reached, of
course. The Play could have led to serious repercussions from the more
conservative factions of Kollek's community, regardless of the claims made
by the producers that their Play was
benign.

Ultimately the diplomacy and resolve of Mr. Kollek prevailed. He
would allow nothing to compromise
his determination that nothing be
done to restrict religious freedom in
Jerusalem. Since the Passion Play did
have a religious basis, it was welcomed.

The Passion Play was welcomed too
by those close to Prime Minister
Menachem Begin, as well as by the Israeli leader himself. The play, they rea-
soned, could advance the cause of better understanding about the
significance of Jerusalem to Jewish history and to Christians and Jews, no
matter where they live today.

The ferocity of Mr. Begin's devotion
to his country is well known and
largely misunderstood. He is not a
megalomaniac as some of his crueler
critics suggest. Nor is he a cold and un-
feeling man. Those closest to him insist that he is compassionate, even dis-
armingly sensitive to the personal
concerns of many.

Begin is a calculating politician, to
be sure. So are most of those who rise
to the top of their national political
structures. What is unusual and grating
to many is his unswerving determination about the Israeli cause. He does
not wish to be known as anything
more than he is: a Jewish patriot, dedicated to the survival of the nation that
he fought for years to establish.

In his memoirs Mr. Begin describes
as great and grave the responsibility
that he and his colleagues have to
"care for the future of the Jewish people, for the safety of the Jewish state,

and for the security and the lives and liberty of our children." That security, he observes, requires a free and united Jerusalem, "without which there can be no security for the State of Israel."

The lessons of the centuries burning in his mind, the Israeli Prime Minister recalls a broadcast he made to the people of the new State of Israel in May 1948. He reminded his listeners then, as he will not let the world forget now: "The homeland is historically and geographically an entity. Whoever fails to recognize our right to the entire homeland does not recognize our right to any of its territories. We shall never yield our natural and eternal right. We shall bear the vision of a full liberation. We shall bear the vision of ultimate redemption, and we shall bring it into realization."

With these words Begin suggests, as most Jews and more recently many Christians are suggesting, that Israel was promised to the Jews by God. Scholars cite many examples of such a prophecy in the Bible, most often from Genesis. In that book the Lord said to Abraham: "Look all round you from where you are towards the north and the south, towards the east and the west. All the land within sight I will give to you and to your descendants for ever."

Prime Minister Begin spoke of this resolve and his interpretation of world affairs during his welcoming address to the thousands of Christians who gathered in Jerusalem for the 1981 Feast of Tabernacles. The affair was arranged and promoted by the International Christian Embassy, an institution created by a clutch of North American and European Christians who are trying to bring a sense of history about Judeo-Christian relations into the contemporary secular world.

Mr. Begin reminded his audience gathered in the Jerusalem convention hall, Biyani HaUma, that if the world thinks all the great decisions about its future are made in Washington, D.C., it is wrong. They have been and will continue to be made, he said, in Jerusalem, D.C.—David's City. The more one considers the Bible, the more one can see Mr. Begin's point. Woe be it to him or her who forgets that the most profound influence on our civilization and its soul has come from the Land of David and of Jesus, who died there for all of us.

That Jerusalem should be the capital of the land of Israel was also prophesied, according to many scholars. For example, they refer to Psalm 132 where it is written: "The Lord has chosen Zion, desiring this to be his home, 'Here I will stay forever, this is the home I have chosen.'"

Whether or not one agrees with these interpretations of the Bible story, those in the higher reaches of government in Washington, Bonn, and London should at least recognize from where it is that the people of Israel come.

In Israel, Araujo and his troupe present their version of the Nativity Play also in Bethlehem. It is a joyous evening of pageant, filled with the great music of the Christmas season. The lighting and direction are a delight to behold. The logistics of staging the Nativity were a great challenge to one and all in the company. Never before has the Christian visitor to the Holy Land had the extraordinary opportunity to experience the re-creation of the birth *and* death of Jesus during the same visit.

But it is the Passion Play that was the focus of attention in Israel and to the producers, for the emotion it generates and for the promise of reconciliation it holds. There is, after all, no question that Jesus was born. It is the way he died and what happened as a result that has been the subject of debate and friction.

The birth of Jesus was sublime. And the event is cause for astonishment and wonder. But it was his death and resurrection that had the more profound effect upon our civilization. In his death Jesus reminded man of his fallibility and helplessness in the absence of God, in the denial of faith. It was the death of Jesus that changed the course of history forever.

After his death and resurrection, the Christian movement really picked up its tempo. Since then most of those things done by his followers, in his name, have been good and constructive. The most disturbing exception to the rule has been the Christian response to the Jew through the centuries. It is an understatement that Judeo-Christian relations have not been good. It is a condition for which there is little excuse. The best that men of good will can do is to examine the causes of the condition and try to reconcile them.

Fortunately for all of us who do seek reconciliation between Christians and Jews, Francisco de Araujo knows his Bible and he is guided by its teaching. This knowledge and faith enabled him to stage successfully the Jerusalem Passion Play—stage it in a way that is satisfying to Christians and engaging to Jews.

How could these productions *fail* to be engaging to the people of Israel, indeed all people with an appreciation for great music, theater, and spectacle tastefully mounted? The Nativity in Bethlehem and Jerusalem Passion Play are great theater. Their natural locations are stunning. The cultural environment provided for them is exhilarating.

After a true and just peace and freedom for all of their people, I detect that the leaders of Israel want a truly vibrant and stimulating cultural life most of all. One needs only remember the contribution of so many Jewish people to the cultural life of other nations to appreciate that desire.

Some time after the closing night in the first season of the Jerusalem Passion Play, I asked Francisco de Araujo about his life in Israel and his reaction to events there. He said that his affection for the land and its people is great. His desire to become even more involved in the cultural scene of the country is intense. He expressed the hope that someday he might be invited to conduct one of Israel's great orchestras. The dedicated Christian also said that he and his lovely wife, Janet, will probably buy a home in Jerusalem. Then, gesturing with the kind of youthful animation that is his way, he said that he was already generating plans to stage other Bible stories in the Holy Land, stories from the Old Testament as well as the New.

It was just beginning to dawn on him that his work in Jerusalem might have a profound effect on many, many people. He knew that his labor and devotion had already profoundly affected those involved in the first season. He reflected in wonder that he had brought together with success Americans, Israelis, and Arabs—Christians, Jews, and Muslims—to produce the plays. It had truly been an international and ecumenical effort.

For me, the writer, the Jerusalem Passion Play has offered an opportunity to be among the people of the Holy Land in the places where Jesus lived and died. I have seen the miracle that is the modern nation of Israel and have experienced firsthand the dedication of that nation to the principles of liberty upon which *my* homeland was founded.

The last time I saw Jerusalem's mayor, Teddy Kollek, I asked him, "If you could send one message to Christians and Jews alike in the United States and Europe, what would it be?" He answered, "Come to Jerusalem and look for yourselves. Don't rely on what the writers say on television and in the newspapers, but look for yourselves."

Francisco de Araujo's achievement may not change the course of history. But it surely is a postscript to history for which he can be justly proud, and for which all of us should be thankful.

Lawrence F. Mihlon
Washington, D.C.
January 1982

Acknowledgments

We are indebted to: The amateur actors, inhabitants of Jerusalem and Bethlehem, who performed the Play and also helped us most generously in our photographic work. They acted with devotion and worked to bring success to our book.

Among the actors we made many friends such as Greg Strom, the interpreter of Jesus. Special thanks to him for his friendly assistance and also for his tremendous effort psychologically and physically during all our work.

Our very special thanks go to Francisco de Araujo, the director and originator of the Play, who helped us relentlessly during our photographic work. His efforts in organizing the entire production so that we could take our photographs were of the utmost generosity. He showed us real friendship. Thank you, Francisco.

And last but not least, our great thanks go to Frank Parsons, the producer of the Plays in Jerusalem and Bethlehem, who by his tremendous personal sacrifice made the whole project possible.

Max and Hilla Jacoby

Not surprisingly, there are many persons to whom I will be grateful always for their time, hard work, and guidance in the creation of this book. Christian, Jew, and Arab; without them this celebration of God's message would not have been possible. Each of them deserves more in writing than space will allow. All I can hope is that they will continue to feel toward me what I will always feel for them: affection and gratitude.

These good people are listed in no particular order because in a work like this each and every contribution somehow seems as important as the others. They are:

Robert Heller, executive editor at Doubleday; his support and diligent action got the project rolling in record time. Amalya Akabus; her good nature helped the Passion Play company to navigate the Tel Aviv–Jerusalem obstacles. Father John Nicholls and David Drummond—the former one of the Queen of England's chaplains, the latter the son of an archbishop; they make me feel better about being an Episcopalian. Dan Pattir, former spokesman for Prime Ministers Itzhak Rabin and Menachem Begin; through him and his counsel the inner sanctum of Israeli democracy was made available.

Zeev Chafets, Uri Porath, and Yehiel Kadashai, counselors to Prime Minister Begin; they gave direction to my search for understanding of Mr. Begin and his government. Bruce Kashdan of the Foreign Office; his friendship lent spirit to the saying, "Next year in Jerusalem."

Wesley Brown and Bernard Resnikoff of Tantur and Ethiopia Street respectively; as bookends they embrace the spirit of reconciliation in the Holy Land. Merv Watson of the International Christian Embassy; his words and music carry great meaning. Joseph Aweidah of the Panorama Hotel; his belief in God bridges the Kidron Valley.

Uzi Pelled of Tel-Ad Studios; he talks my language in English and in Hebrew. Louis C. Kramp and Burt L. Talcott of Washington; they were there at the start.

Max and Hilla Jacoby; more than photographers, they are the embodiment of the Old and New Testaments—thank God we met so many years ago. Francisco and Janet de Araujo, their sponsors and gallant troupers; their willingness to share is credit to him.

Finally, Virginia Donovan of the magic typewriter; her help in preparing the manuscript and her kind words through it all placed the effort in perspective.

Shalom to them all.—LFM

Taking of the Photographs

We used Nikon equipment exclusively. The 80–200mm Zooms were reliable and when desirable we used a normal perspective lens (50mm). When fast shooting and quick adjustment were necessary we kept our equipment as simple as possible. For wide-angle shots we used only 20mm or 35mm lenses. Portrait-type photographs were taken with 85mm lenses. We did not use filters. Different Kodak films were used where appropriate. For all daylight work we used "64" and "200" ASA. When shooting in artificial light we used tungsten "160" ASA. At very low light levels "400" ASA was sufficiently fine-grained in almost all cases. High resolution was important for the shooting of the actual historical sites, so the tripod was set up for the necessary long exposures with very small lens apertures. When taking each photograph we used the entire frame so that a minimum amount of cropping was necessary.